John Young

A criticism on the Elegy written in a country church yard

John Young

A criticism on the Elegy written in a country church yard

ISBN/EAN: 9783337260392

Printed in Europe, USA, Canada, Australia, Japan

Cover: Foto ©Lupo / pixelio.de

More available books at **www.hansebooks.com**

A
CRITICISM
ON THE
ELEGY
WRITTEN IN A
COUNTRY CHURCH YARD.

A

CRITICISM

ON THE

ELEGY

WRITTEN IN A

COUNTRY CHURCH YARD.

BEING A CONTINUATION OF

Dr. J——N's CRITICISM ON THE
POEMS OF GRAY.

———————————

LONDON:

PRINTED FOR G. WILKIE, No. 71, ST. PAUL's
CHURCH YARD.

————

MDCCLXXXIII.

ADVERTISEMENT.

TO prevent any miſtakes that might ariſe, and in juſtice to his Readers and himſelf, the Editor of the following Tract feels himſelf bound to declare, that he has no farther concern in it, than as being accidentally the channel through which it is conveyed to the Public. Having ordered, a few months ago, * Iriſh editions

---

* It is with concern that the Editor has learnt, that this ſpecies of traffic, ſo convenient for the Knights Companions of *the light purſe*, is ſo much at preſent on the decline, as to threaten (in the language of the *Counter*) to be ſpeedily *knocked up*. The *Iriſh* Editors have imprudently *ſcrewed up* their prices too high: and their Rivals on this ſide the water have been, of late, unuſually *ſharp ſet* in running them down, by the aſſiſtance of the Statute Book, and officers of the cuſtoms. It was *a ſorry ſight* to the Editor, laſt vacation, to ſee the Royal warehouſes at the ports oppoſite to the Iriſh coaſt, crowded with ſo many choice and famous Authors, languiſhing in ignoble bonds, and ſome of them expiring, *in defiance of* MAGNA CHARTA, under cruel tortures. . . . Here lay Mrs. C-TH—NE M———Y, juſt new from the *ſheers and ſpunge*,—" her " ſilver ſkin laced with her golden blood,"—pointing to

a
her

editions of some late publications (an irregu-
larity into which the high prices of *town-made*
books, and the low ftate of his own finances,
have fometimes betrayed him, to the detri-
ment of copy-hold rights, and " againft the
" form of the Statute in that cafe provided ;")
he found the parcel, on its arrival in his chambers, to be double-fortified with fwathes of
printed fheets; refembling, in their general
appearance, what is known among the *Trade*,
by the name of *Imperfections*. This, being quite
" *felon les Regles*," excited neither curiofity nor
attention; but approaching, foon after, the
parcel to his teeth, for the purpofe of undoing
the *twine*, the wrappers were again *forced upon
his eye*; when he perceived, by certain cabalif-
tical marks upon the *margins* and *field*, and
which his printer would laugh at him fhould
he attempt to depict, that what he had taken
at firft for imperfections, were no other than
proof-fheets, of a work apparently *critical*, and
which he felicitated himfelf on his chance of
feafting on, perhaps *before* the Public. He fet

her ample gafhes, and bellowing for her HABEAS CORPUS.
. . . There lay the redoubted JUNIUS, his body dif-
membered by the axe, and *his quarters at the King's dif-
pofal*,----and there the ftately G-B-NS, *laniatum corpore toto*,
with the vehicle of his keen elocution *bored through with
red-hot iron*, &c. &c.
    Non, mihi fi linguæ cēntum fint, oraque centum,
    Omnia pœnarum percurrere nomina poffim.
himfelf

himfelf accordingly to examine the fheets with attention; and found them, not without fome furprife, to contain a methodical criticifm upon Gray's " Elegy written in a Country Church-yard;" executed in a manner fomewhat *outré*, and containing Obfervations on certain other Poems of Gray, together with allufions to certain *Analyfes* of them, which were referred to as preceding this particular Criticifm, but which were not to be found in thefe fheets. A fudden thought now entered his head, and one which fome will perhaps think he *too haftily* adopted. Having been lately reading Dr. J-hn—n's Criticifm on Gray (a work which afforded him infinite amufement), and the Doctor's manner being then ftrongly imprefled on his mind, he fancied he perceived a refemblance betwixt the ftyle and mode of Criticifm difplayed in the Doctor's Strictures on Gray's other Poems, and that adopted in the Criticifm now before him. The *leges judicandi* were the fame; and the Editor was led to fancy it poffible, that the Obfervations on the Elegy written in a Country Church-yard, were compofed by Dr. J-hn—n, printed off for publication, along with the other parts of the Criticifm on Gray, but afterwards *withdrawn*; from the fufpicion that a cenfure fo free, of one of the moft popular productions in the Englifh language, might be ill-received by the Public.

Full

Full of this idea, the Editor formed, the refolution of reftoring to his Fellow-Readers what
feemed to him to have been needlefsly taken
away; and thus to gratify their palates with a
difh *that one meets not with every day.*

What his *riper* fentiments upon this fubject
are, the Editor does not chufe to fay. The
Public are in poffeffion of the evidence, both
external and *internal*; and they are left to judge
for themfelves. It is, however, but fair to
admit, that there are fome circumftances which
are rather unfavourable to the idea, that this
Criticifm on Gray's Elegy is the genuine pro-
duction of Dr. J-hn—n. Although it is not difficult to conceive, that means might have been
found to get the * proof-fheets of this work
tranfmitted fucceffively to Ireland (as the proof
fheets of other works have been) *in due courfe of
poft;* and although the cafe of an † Author of

* The great number of proprietors (in all thirty-fix)
whofe names, in eight files, marfhalled in the form of
the CUNEUS, defend the title-page of Dr. J-hn—n's
amufing work, though calculated to ftrike terror in
after pirates, may have even contributed to render eafy
the *firft trefpafs.* Secrecy and Prudence diftributed among
thirty-fix men, become little elfe than *names.* " In the
" multitude of *counfellors* there is fafety:" The cafe is different with *copy-holders.*

† It is faid to be a vouched anecdote of the Author of
" Effays and Treatifes on feveral Subjects," that he revoked
and deftroyed certain Effays, which he had already got
printed off, and in which he found reafon to fufpect that
he had taken his ground rather too haftily.

note,

note, as well as of boldnefs, withdrawing a printed work, previous to the day of publication, is not without precedent in the annals of literature; yet the boldnefs of Dr. J-hn—n is fo COLOSSAL, and his juft confidence in the propriety of his own tafte, and the foundnefs of his critical creed, fo completely INEBRANLABLE, that one may be juftified in doubting, whether it could be poffible for him to bring himfelf to cancel, from prudence, that which he had once printed off for publication. So ftands the argument on *one* fide: but παντι λογω ισος λογος αντικειται; "for every *Rebutter*, there is a *Sur-Rebutter*;" as the fhrewd Sextus has told us.

But whatever may be the Editor's opinion with refpect to the *authenticity* of the Tract now offered to the Public, he finds himfelf at full liberty to acknowledge, that he has more than once repented of the refolution he had formed to reprint it. He foon found that the fheets were in fome places fo faint and blotted, and in others fo erafed and torn, that it was impoffible to prefent it for publication, unlefs in a manufcript copy, taken with much pains, and in which it would be neceffary to call in the aid of *conjecture* towards completing the fenfe by *fupplement* and *interpolation*. Difficult as this appeared in profpect, he found it ftill more difficult in execution: but, though he was often tempted to abandon his enterprize,

Perfeve-

Perfeverance at laſt bore him through the labour he had undertaken. How he has acquit-
ted himſelf in it, it belongs not to him to ſay.
He may have committed miſtakes ; but he has
committed none that he poſſeſſed the means of
avoiding. In one or two proper names, he is
not ſure but he may have ſupplied the defaced
characters *incorrectly*.

From what has been now ſtated, this Tract
muſt neceſſarily be ſuppoſed to meet the Public
eye, in a ſtate ſomewhat different from that in
which it came from the pen of its ſuppoſed Author. The characteriſtic peculiarities of the Writer, and that poignancy which diſtinguiſhes all
his productions, muſt naturally be found in it,
in a *diſguiſed* and *flattened* ſtate ; and the Strictures
muſt have loſt, of courſe, " part of what Tem-
" ple would call their *Race* ; a word which,
" applied to wines, in its primitive ſenſe, means
" the flavour of the ſoil."

It was once intended to print the Criticiſm in a
manner reſembling the editions of *Feſtus*, which
diſtinguiſh, by a difference of character, the
unimpaired paſſages in the original, from the
ſupplements and interpolations. But *technical*
reaſons were adduced againſt this mode ; to
which the Editor was obliged to yield, as he
was not able to refute them. In place of this
contrivance he had ſubſtituted another, which
would have equally gratified the curioſity of
the

the Lovers of the IMITATIVE ARTS, for whofe entertainment this Publication was meant. In imitation of Mr. *Brooke Boothby*, he meant to have depofited the Original in the Britifh Mufeum, for the infpection of the curious. But, alas! the late dreadful conflagration, which extended itfelf in part to his chambers, deprived him of the power of executing what he had planned. The zeal and activity of friends, which faved all his *valuable* property, overlooked thefe dirty fheets. The Editor foon after faw their remains. They had died a gentle death. The flame feemed juft to have reached them at the time its violence was fpent; for they lay undiffipated in a drawer half open, and which was little more than finged. The characters were in part legible, being marked in a pale white, fpreading over a dark ground; furnifhing at once a proof of identity, and claiming a joint appropriation of the character which the Poet had applied exclufively to man:

" EVEN IN OUR ASHES LIVE THEIR WONTED FIRES."

Lincoln's Inn,
15th *Jan.* 1783.

E L E G Y

WRITTEN IN A

COUNTRY CHURCH-YARD.

I.

THE Curfew tolls the knell of parting day *,
The lowing herd winds flowly o'er the lea;
The plowman homeward plods his weary way,
And leaves the world to darkness and to me.

II.

Now fades the glimmering landscape on the fight,
And all the air a folemn ftillnefs holds;
Save where the beetle wheels his drony flight,
And drowfy tinklings lull the diftant folds;

*   —— *The knell of parting day,*]
    —— Squilla di lontano,
Che paia 'l giorno pianger, che fi muore.
                    DANTE, Purgat. l. 8.

b   III.

III.

Save that, from yonder ivy-mantled tower,
The moping Owl does to the Moon complain
Of such, as, wand'ring near her secret bower,
Molest her ancient, solitary reign.

IV.

Beneath those rugged elms, that yew-tree's shade,
Where heaves the turf in many a mould'ring heap,
Each in his narrow cell for ever laid,
The rude forefathers of the hamlet sleep.

V.

The breezy call of incense-breathing Morn,
The Swallow twittering from the straw-built shed,
The Cock's shrill clarion, and the ecchoing horn,
No more shall rouse them from their lowly bed.

VI.

For them no more the blazing hearth shall burn,
Or busy housewife ply her evening care;
No children run to lisp their sire's return,
Or climb his knees the envied kiss to share.

VII.

Oft did the harvest to their sickle yield ;
Their furrow oft the stubborn glebe has broke:
How jocund did they drive their team afield !
How bow'd the woods beneath their sturdy stroke !

VIII.

VIII.

Let not Ambition mock their ufeful toil,
Their homely joys, and deftiny obfcure;
Nor Grandeur hear, with a difdainful fmile,
The fhort and fimple annals of the poor.

IX.

The boaft of heraldry, the pomp of power,
And all that beauty, all that wealth e'er gave,
Await alike th' inevitable hour:
The path of glory leads but to the grave.

X.

Nor you, ye proud, impute to thefe the fault,
If Mem'ry o'er their tomb no trophies raife;
Where, through the long-drawn aifle and fretted
    vault,
The pealing anthem fwells the note of praife.

XI.

Can ftoried urn, or animated buft,
Back to its manfion call the fleeting breath?
Can Honour's voice provoke the filent duft?
Or Flattery footh the dull cold ear of Death?

XII.

Perhaps, in this neglected fpot, is laid
Some heart once pregnant with celeftial fire;
Hands that the rod of empire might have fway'd,
Or wak'd to extacy the living lyre.

b 2   XIII.

XIII.

But Knowledge to their eyes her ample page,
Rich with the fpoils of time, did ne'er unroll;
Chill Penury reprefs'd their noble rage,
And froze the genial current of the foul!

XIV.

Full many a gem of pureft ray ferene
The dark unfathom'd caves' of ocean bear;
Full many a flower is born to blufh unfeen,
And wafte its fweetnefs on the defart air.

XV.

Some village Hampden that, with dauntlefs breaft,
The little tyrant of his fields withftood;
Some mute inglorious Milton here may reft;
Some Cromwell, guiltlefs of his country's blood.

XVI.

Th' applaufe of lift'ning fenates to command,
The threats of pain and ruin to defpife,
To fcatter plenty o'er a fmiling land,
And read their hiftory in a nation's eyes,

XVII.

Their lot forbad: nor circumfcrib'd alone
Their growing virtues, but their crimes confin'd:
Forbad to wade thro' flaughter to a throne,
And fhut the gates of mercy on mankind;

XVIII.

XVIII.

The ftruggling pangs of confcious Truth to hide,
To quench the blufhes of ingenuous Shame,
Or heap the fhrine of Luxury and Pride,
With incenfe kindled at the Mufe's flame.

XIX.

Far from the madding crowd's ignoble ftrife,
Their fober wifhes never learn'd to ftray:
Along the cool fequefter'd vale of life
They kept the noifelefs tenor of their way.

XX.

Yet even thefe bones from infult to protect,
Some frail memorial ftill erected nigh,
With uncouth rhymes and fhapelefs fculpture
    deck'd,
Implores the paffing tribute of a figh.

XXI.

Their name, their years, fpelt by th'unletter'd Mufe,
The place of fame and elegy fupply;
And many a holy text around fhe ftrews,
That teach the ruftic Moralift to die.

XXII.

For who, to dumb forgetfulnefs a prey,
This pleafing anxious being e'er refign'd,
Left the warm precincts of the cheerful day,
Nor caft one longing, lingering look behind?

XXIII.

XXIII.

On some fond breast the parting soul relies,
Some pious drops the closing eye requires:
Even from the grave the voice of Nature cries;
Even in our ashes live their wonted fires *.

XXIV.

For thee, who, mindful of th' unhonour'd dead,
Do'st in these lines their artless tale relate;
If, chance, by lonely contemplation led,
Some kindred Spirit shall enquire thy fate,

XXV.

Haply, some hoary-headed Swain may say,
" Oft have we seen him at the peep of dawn,
" Brushing with hasty steps the dews away,
" To meet the Sun upon the upland lawn.

XXVI.

" There, at the foot of yonder nodding beech,
" That wreathes its old fantastic roots so high,
" His listless length at noontide would he stretch,
" And pore upon the brook that babbles by.

---

* *Even in our ashes live their wonted fires.*]
Ch'i veggio nel pensier, dolce mio fuoco,
Fredda una lingua, et due begli occhi chiusi,
Rimaner dopo noi pien di faville.
PETR. Son. 169.

XXVII.

XXVII.

" Hard by yon wood, now fmiling as in fcorn,
" Mutt'ring his wayward fancies, he would rove;
" Now drooping, woeful wan, like one forlorn,
" Or craz'd with care, or crofs'd in hopelefs love.

XXVIII.

" One morn I mifs'd him on the cuftom'd hill,
" Along the heath, and near his favourite tree:
" Another came; nor yet befide the rill,
" Nor up the lawn, nor at the wood was he.

XXIX.

" The next, with dirges due, in fad array,
" Slow thro' the church-way path we faw him
    " born.
" Approach and read (for thou can'ft read) the lay,
" Grav'd on his ftone beneath yon aged thorn.".

THE EPITAPH.

XXX.

Here refts his head upon the lap of Earth,
A youth to Fortune, and to Fame unknown :
Fair Science frown'd not on his humble birth;
And Melancholy mark'd him for her own.

XXXI.

XXXI.

Large was his bounty, and his foul fincere;
Heav'n did a recompence as largely fend:
He gave to Mifery all he had,—a tear;
He gain'd from Heav'n ('twas all he wifh'd) a Friend.

XXXII.

No farther feek his merits to difclofe,
Or draw his frailties from their dread abode,
(There they alike in trembling hope repofe *),
The bofom of his Father, and his God.

---

* *(There they alike in trembling hope repofe,)*]
——— paventofa fpeme.   PETR. Son. 114.

MY procefs has brought me at laft to the far-famed " Elegy written in a Country Church-yard." Of this Elegy, Caution feems to dictate, that Cenfure fhould fay but little, where Praife has faid fo much. Even Obfti-nacy is content to admit it to be poffeffed of the prefumptive claim to commendation, which is derived from popularity. Literary hiftory furnifhes not many inftances, where the anxie-ties of authors have been fully removed, before the Public was in poffeffion of their work. Yet fuch was the cafe in the inftance before us. The favourable opinion of the world, with re-fpect to this poem, was afcertained whilft it was yet *in the birth*; and Attention was roufed by repeated whifpers, about a capital elegiac pro-duction, circulating among a few confidential friends, and of whofe author it was faid (in the cant ufual on fuch occafions) that the diffi-dence withheld it from the public eye. In fuch fituations there are never wanting encouragers to *cocker and fpirit up* the modeft author; who yields at laft to importunity, and the dread of a mutilated and furreptitious publication. It is however but fair to confefs, that on this occafion the folicitations of Gray's friends were not merely complimentary. The recital of certain brilliant ftanzas had fecured approbation to the whole. Praife in this inftance *preceded* publication, as in fome other inftances he found it follow far behind ; and Gray felt himfelf in a fituation fingular among authors ; not foliciting public favour, but folicited to accept it.

The Elegy written in a Country Church Yard has become a *ftaple* in Englifh poetry. It is even beginning to *get into years*. Of thofe that now frequent the haunts of them that make verfes, or that judge of them, the greater part remember not the time when it was not recited with approbation : and when a few laggers, who witneffed its firft introduction, and heard now and then a tone of diffent interrupting the notes of admiration, fhall have *fretted their hour*, and away, the cuftom of praifing it will be entitled to the denomination of a *good cuftom*, which, in criticifm as well as law, holds of prefcription ; being " that whereof the memory of man runneth not to the contrary."

Though

Though the curiosity of the Public had done
nothing to push forward this Elegy, Sagacity
might easily have foreseen its success. Meditation upon death is, and ever has been, the
occasional business or pastime of mankind; and
though, like devotion, it cannot admit of the
sublimer flights of poetry, yet, when the mind
has fairly clung to the subject with its senfibilities awakened, and their expressions within
call, nothing that is thus produced will be to-
tally void of interest. The views, if not striking from novelty, will be commanding from
seriousness: and even mediocrity in the senti-
ment will be a passport to general correspond-
ence.

The delusion too under which Gray laboured, that his character was a pensive one, and
which, though not permanent, was periodical,
seems to have lent its aid towards fitting him
for compositions of this kind. The frequent
recurrence of any propensity leads, by sure
steps, to the final adjustment of the character;
and even when the propensity is ideal, the repetition of the fits will, in the end, invest Fancy
with the habitudes of Nature. Whatever part
self-deception or affectation may have originally had in the matter; Gray became, at
length, *bona fide*, a melancholy man. The features of his mind plied gradually to the cast of
the mould his imagination had formed for it.

Of

Of the language of the feeling he became poffeffed of a competent portion, as well as of its
modes, to which, on feveral occafions, he gave
expreffion ; and on none more remarkably,
than in compofing the Elegy under confideration.

If, in eftablifhing the fortune of literary pro-
duations, Popularity eftablifhed alfo their worth,
Criticifm would find herfelf rid of one of the
moft unpleafing, as well as unprofitable, of her
tafks. But this is not the cafe. The maxim
" Vox Populi, &c." taken in its full range, is
not more deftruative to good government, than
hurtful to found criticifm. To examine the
Elegy written in a Country Church Yard, fo as
to reft its merits upon firm ground, its popularity fhould be kept out of view. Of fuch an
examination the objea is not to difcover what
has been faid, but what *may* be faid juftly.
Criticifm aas not in the charaaer of *Recorder*,
but of *Judge*. It is not her bufinefs to EN-
GROSS decifions, but to DICTATE them.

Of this Elegy I find little in the " General
Defign," either to praife or to blame. It
differs in nothing material from the general
defign of all Meditations on Death, from Boyle
to Hervey inclufive. The fubjea has the ad-
vantage of being interefting, but the difadvan-
tage of being common. The reader attends
to it from motives of duty as well as of intereft.

So

.So does alfo the writer: though he foon finds that piety confers not poetic infpiration, and that fublimity is not the neceffary offspring of a ferious frame. The paucity of the topics precludes circumvagation; and the innovelty of the views reprefs effufion. The fubject is already as great as it can be made: and of decoration the execution would be difficult, and the experiment attended with danger.

Of the " Particular Plan," Criticifm withholds the cenfure, until fhe fhall have afcertained the conception. Perhaps the author had no particular plan at all. A number of different views of the fubject, all of them ferious, moft of them common, and many of them interefting, are collected from different quarters, and thrown together in that inconfecutive train, in which men meditate, when they meditate for themfelves. " *Ibi hæc incondita folus.*" Like Virgil's Corydon (who is deprived of fympathy from the bafenefs of his object, as the poet is of his praife, from degrading his foliloquy into a *paftoral)* the Meditator in the Country Church-yard is fuppofed to touch on the different topics as they arife to his mind, not prefcribing the law of fucceffion, but receiving it.

Of poets who had wrought on the fubject before him, either incidentally or from purpofe, he feems to have followed no one completely

pletely as a model, but to have gathered occafionally from all. Parnell's Night-Piece feems
to have been moft in his eye: though of Parnell
the fcheme is, in much, different from that of
Gray. From Milton's *Penferofo* too he has
taken feveral hints; and what may appear furprifing, fome even from his *Allegro*. From
Thomfon and Collins he has been furnifhed
with many images; and fome thoughts are
borrowed from Pope. Materials brought together from fo many different quarters, may be
expected to form an heterogeneous whole.
Adherence is not folidity: and we look not for
a rigorous unity in a *cento*.

Of the "verfification" I delay the ftrict examination, until my procefs fhall have brought me
to the particular paffages that fuggeft it. Only,
in general, it may be doubted, whether the
quatrain with alternate rhimes, has that connexion with the elegiac ftrain that many poets
and fome critics have conceived. Dryden,
who was eminent in both characters, is fo clearly
of opinion that it is the moft *magnificent* of
Englifh meafures, that one is apt to wonder
how it fhould have firft been thought of as a
vehicle for a fpecies of poetry, of which the
character is *gentlenefs* and *tenuity*. It is the
ftanza adopted by Hammond. But the credit
of Hammond's poetry was not of magnitude
fufficient to give a claffical ftamp to any kind
of

of verſification. Mr. Maſon thought more
favourably of his friend's authority ; and by his
advice Gray was prevailed on to uſe the quatrain, that the merit and eminence of this poem
might ſecure to Elegy the excluſive and un-
diſturbed poſſeſſion of that meaſure.

Such was the idea of Mr. Maſon, of whoſe
ſagacity in foreſeeing events, the reader, from
his ſuccefs in this, may form no unfavourable
idea. Yet of this meaſure it may be ſaid with
truth, that it brings with it no momentous
acceſſion to the powers of Engliſh verſification.
It poſſeſſes all the imperfections of blank verſe,
acquired with all the labour of rhime. The
coincidences of terminating ſound, by being
alternate, admit of an interruption by which
they are either loſt, or found at the expence
of a labour greater than the gratification they
bring : and the ſtanza, by being limited to a
certain definite compaſs, either forces the poet
to end his thought abruptly, or to eke it out
with ſupplemental and expletive matter, always
weakening expreſſion, and rarely concealing
diſtrefs. It is ſomewhat ſurpriſing that blank
verſe, improper in almoſt all other ſubjects,
ſhould never have been thought of as a vehicle
for that ſpecies of excurſive thinking which
prevails ſo much in the elegiac ſtrain. Young
has uſed it with ſuccefs in his great work,

which

which, in diffufion and defultorinefs, approaches to the nature of the Elegy.

Criticifm never feels herfelf more keenly actuated with the fenfe of humiliation, than when fhe is laid under the neceffity of extending her ftriftures to margins and title-pages. Yet circumftances will, at times, occur, to make fuch degradation indifpenfable. Of the poem now under confideration, the title might have efcaped cenfure, had it not been originally different from what it now is ; and had not the author perfuaded himfelf to fuppofe, that when he altered it he mended it of courfe. It is feldom that the change of a title is a happy change. If it has had a feat in the imagination previous to the operation of compofing, or even during its progrefs, it has confiderably influenced the execution. It has fo led and regulated the train of thinking, and the mutual dependencies, that the flighteft after-deviation from it is in danger of creating inconfiftency. It introduces a fpecies of confufion and inconfequence like that which was introduced into the Dunciad, when Pope, at the inftigation of Warburton †, changed the hero of that piece ; and which, tho' both the poet and his Mentor kept botching at it during the whole of their

† Bowyer.—It is to be hoped that the executors of this gentleman will take fome method of preventing from perifhing the much curious information which his profeffion and induftry enabled him to colleft.

lives,

lives *, they were not able to remove; though the labour of Procruftes was doubled, and both the tortured and inftruments of torture were racked to produce accommodation.

Gray has more than once been unfortunate in his fancy of changing his titles. He had compofed an Ode, to which he gave the title of *Noon-Tide*. Falling out of humour with this title afterwards, for what reafon does not appear, he † new-chriftened it an " Ode on Spring." Noon-tide, however, was in his imagination, when he wrote it, and it is an Ode on Noon-tide ftill.

" Reflexions in a Country Church-Yard" was ‡ the title by which this piece was firft known; a title plain, fober, and expreffive of its nature; but too undignified, in the apprehenfion of its Author, who perfuaded himfelf to think " Elegy" a nicer name. He fhould, however, have confidered that, in adopting the new title, he fubjected himfelf to feverer rules of criticifm than before; and fhut himfelf out from many pleas in defence or palliation of its defultory ftyle, which would have been open to him from its old title of " Reflexions;" a

* Pope did not long furvive the change. In the private correction of Warburton, I find little that can create regret for that precaution of the Poet, which prevented them from being made publick.

† Mafon,   ‡ Mafon.

C   title

title in which little unity being promifed, there
is little right to expect it. Being completely
put together too, before the change of title
took place, and fuffered, after the change, to
remain in a great meafure as before, it became
charged with incongruities too obvious to
efcape obfervation. Though an Elegy *may* be
written in a Church-yard, as well as in a clofet,
and in a *Country* Church-yard even better than
in a *Town* one; yet courtefy itfelf muft pro-
nounce it fantaftical, if an Elegy *is* to be written, to chufe out a place for writing it, where
the conveniencies for that operation are a wanting, and where even the common implements
either exift not at all, or exift by premedita-
tion. Who is there that fays, or would be
endured to fay, " I will take me pen, ink and
" paper, and get me out into a church-yard,
" and there write me an elegy; for *I do well to*
" *be melancholy?*" Parnell has carried the matter
far enough, when he refolves to get out into a
church-yard, and *think* melancholy thoughts.

If the writers of ftudied ferioufnefs, and
recorders of premeditated griefs, would em-
ploy one half of the time fpent in preparing
their fadneffes for the public eye, in examining
into the propriety of introducing them to the
public at all, the journals of poetry would be
lefs difgraced than they are with the *balance* of
of affectation againft nature. The ferioufnefs,

which

which embraces the heart, is not the offspring
of volition, but of inftinct. It is not a purpofe, but a frame. The forrow, that is forrow indeed, afks for no prompting. It comes
without a call. It courts not admiration. It
preffes not on the general eye; but haftens
under covert, and wails its widowhood alone.
Its ftrong-hold is the heart. There it remains
clofe curtained; *unfeeing, unfeen*. Delicacy and
tafte recoil at the publications of internal griefs.
They profane the hallowednefs of fecret fad-
nefs; and fuppofe felected and decorated expreffion compatible with the proftration of the
foul.

Not only are they indelicate, and out of nature : they are alfo imprudent. Sadnefs is a
tranfient feeling. The violence of its effufions
produces its expenditure, as the agitation of
fluids promotes their evaporation. Of its firft
unreafonablenefs, when the expreffion is only
oral, little harm is done; for the language is
perifhable as the feeling: but " *litera fcripta
manet* ;" and when the man whom " melancholy had marked for his own" is found, in
violation of his vow, " tripping on light fantaftic toe," or the inconfolable hufband who
was to cherifh no fecond flame, confents to
comfort himfelf in one wife for the lofs of another, they find the public in poffeffion of their

written

written wailings, and not a little out of temper
with them, that they have not kept their word.
Of the firft Lord Littleton, there are many
fimple men of feeling who have fcarcely brought
themfelves to believe, even on the authority of
the Regifter, that, after the death of his Lucy,
he married a.fecond wife. Enough of this.

To the incongruities already fpecified, may
be added another in this Elegy, invefted as it
is with its prefent title; and that other yet
more flagrant. Gray had originally laid his
Meditation, at a time with which the idea of
the operation of writing was incompatible.
The " parting day;" the " glimmering landfcape fading on the fight;" the " plowman
returning home, and leaving the world to darknefs;" are images cohfiftent with the fuppofi-
tion of a *thinking* mufer, but irreconcileable
with the procefs of *writing,* or even fcrawling.
Yet by a friend of Gray, a ferious, and not
unintelligent perfon, who has put together
verfes himfelf, and to whom I communicated
this obfervation, have I been called upon to
take notice, that the Author has defcribed himfelf, in the Elegy, as carrying on his mufing
by moon-light.

* * * * * * * * * *

I,

I. II. III.

Of this Elegy the three firſt quatrains preſent what may be termed the *preparation.* To
the ſerious exercife that is to take place, it is
neceſſary, that the *ſenſes* be firſt properly got
under ; or at leaſt that ſuch work be cut out
for them, as may prevent them from embroil-
ing the train of penſive thought. With propriety then has the Author made them the
objects of his firſt care. With propriety too,
are *hearing* and *ſight* ſelected ; as the moſt ref-
tive, and unfriendly to meditation, and, of
courſe, requiring management the moſt. Gray
has puſhed this matter a point farther. Not
contented with their neutrality, he has proceeded to court their aſſiſtance ; and held out to
them ſuch " *guerdons fair,*" as might win them
not only not to obſtruct meditation, but to act
as auxiliaries in promoting it.

When theſe guerdons are brought forward in
review; for the *ear* we have " the ſound of the
curfew ;" " the lowing of the herds, returning

to their ftalls ;" " the tinkling (I fuppofe) of
wether-bells ;" " the droning of the beetle ;"
and " the fcreeching of the owl ;" founds
not improper when taken fingly, but deftruc-
tive when taken in the total, to that *folemn
ftilnefs* which is fpoken of. We are tempted
to think of Hogarth's " enraged Mufician,"
whofe rapture is deftroyed by an agglomeration
of founds, each of which, taken feparately,
might have been with patience endured.

For the *eye* we are prefented with " the flow
winding off of the cattle ; " the plodding pace
of the returning plowman ;" " the fading of
the landfcape ;" and " the moon, difcovering
by her light a tower mantled with ivy." Of
thefe images, criticifm is content to admit
the propriety, whilft fhe denies their originality ; and referves to herfelf the right of ftric-
ture on the plan, according to which they are
affembled, and the manner in which they are
drawn.

If the images above recited are traced to
the poets from whom they are taken, we fhall
not always perceive them to have found their
way into the Elegy written in a Country Church-
yard, in an *improved* ftate. Of the curfew, as
heard by a man of meditation, we have the
following circumftantiation in Milton's Penferofo ;

Oft, on a plat of rifing ground,
I hear the *far-off* curfew found ;.
Over fome wide-water'd fhore
Swinging flow with fullen roar.

To this characteriftical figuring Gray has thought
proper to fubftitute the conceit of *Dante*; according to which the curfew is made to toll
requiems to the day newly deceafed : a fancy
more fubtle than folid, and to which the judgment, if reconciled at all, is reconciled by
effort.

Of Evening the approach is defcribed in the
Elegy, as a profe-mufer would have defcribed
it : " The glimmering landfcape fades on the
fight;" let us hear Thomfon :

A faint erroneous ray,
Glanc'd from th' imperfect furfaces of things,
Flings *half an image* on the ftraining eye ;
While wavering woods and villages and ftreams
And rocks——are all one fwimming fcene,
Uncertain if beheld †.

Or, more comprefs'd in the thought, and invefted with the fweetnefs of rhime ;

But chief, when evening fhades decay,
And *the faint landfcape fwims away*,
Thine is the *doubtful foft decline*,
And that beft hour of mufing thine ‡.

† Summer.   ‡ Ode to Solitude.

And Collins:

> Be mine the hut that views
> —Hamlets brown, and dim-difcover'd fpires,
> And hears their fimple bell, and marks, o'er all,
>   Thy dewy fingers draw
>   The gradual dufky veil *.

The idea of making *founds* of a certain kind give a *relief* (to fpeak in the language of ar-tifts) to *filence*, is not new. Thus wrote Collins in 1746:

> Now air is hufh'd, fave where the weak-ey'd bat,
> With fhort fhrill fhriek, flits by on leathern wing;
>   Or, where the beetle winds
>   His fmall, but fullen horn †.

The beetle of Collins and Gray is the "*grey fly*" of Milton, that in the penfive man's ear " winds his fultry horn." Collins has changed the epithet into *fullen*, by a happy *mifremem-brance*.

In Parnell, in place of " ivy mantling a tower," we have " yew bathing a charnel-houfe with dew." The ivy and the tower might ftand any where as well as in a church-yard; but the charnel-houfe is characteriftic, and the yew is funereal. Of Parnell's image, however, candor muft acknowledge the ftrength to be fo great as to render it almoft offenfive.

---

* Ode to Evening.   † Ibid.

In Gray the introduction of the Owl is proper. Parnell's Ravens might have found another place to croak in than a church-yard, and another time than night. But the *part* the Owl acts in the Elegy is impertinent and foolish ; and exhibits an example of a writer spoiling a fine image, by *piecing* it. On some fine evening Gray had seen the moon shining on a tower such as is here described. An owl might be peeping out from the ivy with which it was clad : Of the observer, the station might be such, that the Owl, now emerged from the mantling, presented itself to his eye in profile, skirting with the Moon's limb. All this is well. The perspective is striking : and the picture well defined. But the poet was not contented. He felt a desire to enlarge it : And, in executing his purpose, gave it accumulation without improvement. The idea of the Owl's *complaining* is an artificial one ; and the views on which it proceeds absurd. Gray should have seen, that it but ill befitted the *Bird of Wisdom* to complain to the Moon of an intrusion, which the Moon could no more help than herself.

I suspect this idea, of the Owl complaining to the Moon, to have been a borrowed one, though I do not certainly know from whom. Addison, whose piety deterred him from doubting that Religion was capable of poetic

embellishembellifhment, has made the Moon tell a ftory, and the Stars and Planets fing a devotional catch *. But of fancies approaching to Gray's, I find no one that approaches fo clofely, as that contained in the children's book, where the little dog is drawn *barking at the moon.* It is expoftulation in the one cafe, and fcolding in the other. Gray has chofen the moft refpect-ful. But enough of this. Criticifm is content to check a curiofity that wants an adeqnate ob-ject, and would fpare Poetry the mortification of finding herfelf tracked to the lanes and blind allies where her trappings were firft picked up.

Though the complaint of the Owl is unrea-fonable, her diftrefs is characteriftical, and prettily expreffed; yet " bower" is rather a gay term for an Owl's eyry; and of the ap-plication of " reign," where there are none to reign over, the propriety admits of doubt.

A few words more on the *expreffion*, in thefe three ftanzas. " Leaves the world to darknefs and to me," is quaint, and puts us in mind of great Anna, who

Does fometimes *counfel* take, and fometimes *tea* † ;

but quaintnefs is what every reader comes prepared to meet with in Gray. It is one of the moft marked features in his poetical cha-racter, and fometimes extends to his profe ‡.

* Spectator, N° 465.   † Pope.   ‡ Mafon's Collection.

" I am

" I am come," (fays he, in one of his letters
to his friend) " to *town*, and *better hopes of feeing
you*." " How *little* are the *Great*," was the clofing line of a ftanza in that Ode *, where.it is
faid, that " they that creep and they that fly,
fhall *end* where they *began :*" and fo he fuffered
it for fome time to ftand, in application, no
doubt, of his own idea of a clofing thought,
which ought, as he expreffes himfelf †, " to
have a flower ftuck in it," or " to be twirled
off into an apophthegm." The flower, however, in time, ceafed to pleafe him : yet, with
fo faultering a hand did he pluck it out, and
fo awkwardly did he re-adjuft the parts that
remained, that, as his Editor obferves, the
change was for the worfe, and the thought loft
its original poignancy ‡.

When I am told that " all the Air a folemn
ftillnefs holds," I hefitate, and endeavour to
difcover which of the two is the holder, and
which is the held. If it is the *Air* that holds
the ftillnefs, too great liberty is taken with the
verb ; and if it is the ftillnefs that holds the
Air, the action is too violent for fo quiet a perfonage : but the found was neceffary, to affift
the bell-wedders to complete the lulling of the
folds.

---

* Ode on Spring.   † Mafon.   ‡ Ibid.

        Having

Having cleared the way in the preceding ftanzas, he now enters upon his ground, and lays out his Church-yard in form. Here Criticifm is pofed, unable to anfwer the queftion, " What is the moft proper Church-yard ?" Whether there be *a Tafte* in Church-yards ; and a felection of *Capabilities* required in this, as well as in other modifications of terrene furface, I am uncertain. Nor do I know that Kent, or the other Englifh architects, ever laid out a Church-yard ; though it appears that the Scotch, who are eager to make the moft of every thing, have taken even *that* into their general plan of * pleafure ground. Gray's Church-yard has been defigned : But the fancy of Cipriani, wedded to the foftnefs of Bartolozzi, has not been able to produce from it any thing that makes a decifive appeal to any one feeling of the heart.

Neither of Parnell, nor of Gray, does the Church-yard contain any thing that any church-yard might not contain. Of Parnell, the Church-yard and its environs are thus prefented to the Reader's view. " In diftant profpect, a lake : " refting on its bofom, the Moon, furround- " ed by Stars, having for ground a fky deep " azure: on the right, rifing grounds, "*retiring* " *in dimnefs from the fight :*" on the left, the " Church-yard ; or (as he, in imitation of the

---

* Called by them Policy.

" Hebrew

" Hebrew fimplicity, calls it) the *Place of*
" *Graves*, furrounded by a wall, which is lav-
" ed by a filent ftream : a fteeple, belonging
" no doubt to the Church : a charnel-houfe,
" over-canopied with yew : graves, with their
" turf ofier-bound : other graves, with fmooth
" flat ftones infcribed : and others ftill, fplen-
" didly done out with marble, &c."

Gray's Church-yard is thus connected with
its adjuncts, and prefented to the Reader's eye.
" In near profpect, a Village : herds and la-
" bourers returning home : glimmering land-
" fcape : tower ivy-mantled, having for creft
" an owl, in profile and perfpective, fkirting
" the moon : rugged elms : fhady yew : an
" old thorn ; and the furface fwelling here
" and there with common graves. Hard by is
" a wood, a nodding beach, and a brook
" running over pebbles."

Of the two Defigns, taken in a general view,
that of Parnell feems the more perfect. The
affemblage takes in every thing that a Church-
yard fhould contain ; and a *gradation* of graves
is introduced, with due attention to the diftinction of ranks, which is not loft even in a
Church-yard. In this refpect Gray's Church-
yard is imperfect, and the imperfection has
deprived his meditation of fome of its intereft.
It has, befides, no charnel-houfe. In other
refpects it is much as it fhould be, which, at

6   beft,

beft, is but a negative merit. The abfence of blemifh is not perfection : and of that Officer, fmall will be the claim to praife, who, complying with the rule of the fervice, comes out to mount guard in his regimentals.

———————

IV.

Of inaccuracy in the formation of the thought, the fourth quatrain furnifhes fome examples. It is more according to truth, as well as convenience, to fuppofe a Church-yard *hedged round* with trees, than *planted* with them. A Church-yard is not a thicket. A human body buried at the foot of a large tree, with ftrong fpreading roots, is more confonant to poetry, than to practice. It is not true, that in an ordinary affemblage of graves, the " turf heaves in mouldering heaps." If the ground heaves, no doubt the turf will heave with it : but the " heaps," if they are " *mouldering* heaps," muft heave *through* the turf, not the turf *in* them. " Rude forefathers of the hamlet," is equivocal. The forefathers of a hamlet fhould mean other, ancienter hamlets. But of hamlets there are no genealogies. Among them no degrees of confanguinity are reckoned.

V.

―――――――

V. VI.

The two following ſtanzas contain a paraphraſe of the two laſt lines of the preceding; viz.

> Each in his narrow cell for ever laid,
> The rude forefathers of the hamlet ſleep.

And of this Paraphraſe it may be granted
that the language is pleaſing; but of the circumſtances brought into view, there is no
pointed and reſpective application to the different orders of dead that are ſpecified. Though
the ſleepers are ſubjected to claſſification, and
diſtinguiſhed into four ſets, Reapers, Tillers,
Team-drivers, and Wood-cutters; and though
the Rouſers to morning labour are alſo enu-
merated as four; yet the departments are not
ſet off diſtinctly, nor are the ſounds that are to
rouſe, characteriſtically appropriated to each.
Neither the " twittering of the ſwallow," nor
the " clarion of the cock," have reference to
one ſet of ſleepers more than to another: and
the " echoing horn" ſeems to have nothing
to do with any of them. What is meant by
the " breezy call of incenſe-breathing morn,"
as an help to early riſing, is not very plain:
though this is one of the lines that it is thought
creditable to apprehend and feel.

Thom-

Thomſon, indeed, has aſked the following
queſtion :

> Falſely luxurious, will not man ariſe,
> And, ſpringing from the bed of ſloth, enjoy
> The *cool*, the *fragrant*, and the ſilent hour * ?

But the motive contained in this expoſtulation
is not phyſical, but moral ; it is directed to
thoſe that are already awake, but who, from
lazineſs, continue a-bed, when they ſhould be
ſtirring about.

" Twitter," applied to the ſwallow, is one of
thoſe words whoſe meaſure and articulation are
ſuppoſed to reſemble what they denote. Gray
found it in Dryden ; and, as Thomſon had
done before him, took it on truſt. But what
ſhall we ſay of the " *clarion* of the cock ?" It is
no doubt allowed to Poetry to exalt the little,
by comparing it to the great ; but, *ſunt certi
fines.* To ſwell out an inſignificant little animal, by an accumulation of glaring trappings ;
and to compare his little ſhrill pipe to a bold
inſtrument of martial muſic, is to ſubject the
animal, as well as the deſcription, to contempt.
Incredulus odi.

When Cupid, in an Ode of Anacreon, gives
the name of winged Dragon to a Bee, and calls

* Summer.

the

the puncture received from his fting a " mortal
wound," the levity of the piece, as well as the
defign, reconciles us to the hyperbole. In
making his grey fly " wind a horn," Milton has
gone fully as far as he ought. It is not enough
for the juftification of Gray, that his offence
is not greater than Milton's ; that " clarion"
is not more to the cock, than " horn" is to the
beetle. The juftnefs of poetical defcription
has nothing to do with the doctrine of ratios.
Hamlet's advice concerning chafte playing,
applies equally to chafte defcription. There
may be an " outftepping the modefty of nature" in both.

If " ftraw-built fhed" be meant as defcrip-
tive of a fwallow's neft, it is an affected expreffion, and adopted in defiance of obfervation.
A fhed is a roof or covering : the roof or covering has, in the cafe of a fwallow's neft, nothing to do with ftraw ; nor is it built by the
fwallow at all.

In the fixth ftanza we are told, that the
" blazing hearth burns :" although it is obvious, that the hearth neither blazes nor burns;
but the fire *upon* the hearth. But more than
this might be forgiven to the picture of do-
meftic happinefs which the ftanza holds out,
and which is drawn with great intereft, and
much fimplicity.

E   Thom-

Thomſon had ſaid, in a caſe ſomewhat ſimi-
lar,

> In vain for him th' officious wife prepares
> The fire fair blazing, and the veſtment warm ;
> In vain his little children, peeping out
> Into the mingling ſtorm, demand their fire,
> With tears of artleſs innocence. Alas !
> Nor wife nor children more ſhall he behold,
> Nor friends, nor ſacred home *.

Here are the ſame images.   The blazing fire ;
the buſy wife plying her evening care ; and the
children anxious for their father's return. They
occur alſo in nearly the ſame order.   The
image of the children, however, Gray has improved by the addition of a tender ſtroke not
in the original :

> Nor climb his knees the envied kiſs to ſhare,

VII. VIII.

In the ſeventh quatrain is contained the diſ-
criminated catalogue of the dead, already alluded to ; and in the eighth, the *caveat* to
grandeur and ambition. Of this latter ſtanza,
however, the laſt two lines ſerve little other
purpoſe than to complete the number to four.

* Winter.

The

The idea was already fully in our poffeffion.
" Grandeur" is but "Ambition" in his Sunday's
clothes: Ambition's " mockery," and Grandeur's " difdainful fmile," are the fame: and
the " fhort; but fimple annals of the poor,"
are their " ufeful toil; homely joys; and obfcure deftiny." But this is a fault chargeable
on Gray throughout the whole Elegy. In
every defcription we recognize the rhetorician;
ftudioufly prefenting his object in a multitude
of different afpects, and creating an artificial
encreafe of dimenfion by a minute and tedious
enumeration.

IX.

In the three firft lines of the ninth ftanza is
inculcated a ferious truth, by way of check to
the fneers of grandeur and ambition. But
Beauty is forced awkwardly into the company of
thefe fcoffers. As fhe was no accomplice in
their mockery, fhe is unjuftly, as well as un-
politely; involved in their mortification. Of
the third line the expreffion is faulty, becaufe
it is obfcure. The fignification of the word
" await," is not yet pointedly afcertained.

Whe-

Whether does the hour of death await pomp and beauty; or do they await it? Both modes of phrafeology have examples in our language.

> Even as the wretch, condemn'd to lofe his life,
> Awaits the falling of the murderous knife;

is faid by Fairfax. But the other is the more generally received ufage. We rather accuftom ourfelves to fay, that "the evil awaits the fufferer;" than that "the fufferer awaits the evil." According to this view, it fhould be *awaits*. But as by this means the nominative and the verb would change places, and the arrangement be awkward to an Englifh ear; in feveral editions, and particularly in Mr. Mafon's, it has been printed "await." There is a difficulty both ways. When in the ufe of any expreffion, an author finds himfelf fo pinched and befet, he ought to abandon it altogether, and fubftitute one of more extenfive capability.

The ftanza concludes with a conceit. It is not true, that "the path of glory leads *but* to to the grave." Nor is it *becaufe* it is the path of glory that it leads thither at all. Parnell's thought, with lefs conceit, has in it more of intereft, and much more of piety.

> Death's but a path that muft be trod,
> If man would ever pafs to God *.

* Night-Piece.

In

In a feries of ftanzas that follow, the Author fets himfelf to expoftulate with the proud; and undertakes to prove the abfurdity of the contempt which he fuppofes them ready to pour on the " unhonoured dead;" for their want of more fuperb monuments, from a regular fucceffion of *common places*.

1. It was no fault of theirs that they had them not.
2. They would have ftood them in little ftead.
3. Worth and genius may be without them.
4. It was the injuftice of fortune that made them want them.
5. The account was balanced for them another way.

All which topics are handled with decent plaufibility, and at decent length.

X.

It is in the tenth ftanza that this train of thought commences. But the introduction is not clear of incumbrance. " Impute not to thefe the fault," is an affected and inadequate expreffion for " don't treat them with fcorn." The two laft lines are the moft majeftic in the whole Elegy. But they contain an appeal to feelings, which none but thofe who are fo hap-

4   py

py as to have been bred up in a veneration for
the folemn forms and fervice of the National
Church, can expect to poffefs; The palate of
a Sectary, accuftomed to the reception of flender foods, will naufeate the full meal fet before him in thefe lines:

Where thro' the long-drawn ifle, and fretted vault;
The pealing anthem fwells the note of praife.

Of this laft line, however, Criticifm muft remark;
that either the compofition of the thought is
faulty, or the arrangement of the expreffion is
inverted; It is not the anthem that fwells the
note, but the agglomeration of notes that fwells
the anthem; I am content to fuppofe this to
have been his meaning; communicated in a
mode of arrangement, unpleafing to an Englifh reader in his own language, but of which
he admits the propriety in Latin compofitions.
I have feen this line moft correctly transferred
into that language in many different modes;
all of them meritorious, in a collection of ex-
ercifes written by the Boys of the firft form in
Merchant Taylor's School, and fent to me with
a view, of which I will not gratify my vanity
with the publication; though juftice requires
that of the worthy mafter I fhould folace the
labours, by recording the unwearied diligence;
and by bearing teftimony to thofe abilities that

are

are exerted in forming the *rifing hopes* of an‑
other age.

———————————

XI.

Fault has already been found with Gray for
conforming to the affected ufe of participles in
place of adjectives. " Honied fpring;" " mad‑
ding crowd, &c." " Storied urn ;" is of the
fame family, and even more exceptionable, be‑
caufe liable to mifapprehenfion. The meaning
of the epithet is, " having ftories figured upon it."
In the Penferofo of Milton it is to be found as
an epithet applied to windows, of which the panes
are of painted glafs. It is alfo ufed by Pope.
" Flattery foothing the *ear* of death," is cha‑
racteriftical. What is faid of " honour's voice"
is not faid happily. There is a want of appro‑
priation. " Silent duft," is one of thefe expref‑
fions, which Voltaire ufed to denominate *des
Suiffes*; always ready at a call, and willing to
engage in any fervice.

———————————

XII. XIII.

In the two following quatrains is well de‑
fcribed the depreffion of genius under ignorance
and

and poverty. But here too allowance muſt be made for a little of the *old leaven*. Hands are, *metaphorically*, ſaid to " ſway the rod of empire," and *literally* to bring forth ſounds from the lyre. " Living lyre" is from Cowley ; and of his obligation to the royal poet of Judah, for the application of the idea " awake" to the eliciting of ſounds from the harp or lyre, he has thought the acknowledgment deſerving commemoration. In the whole of the Elegy, Criticiſm has not been able to find two more happy lines than the following :

> Chill penury repreſs'd their noble rage,
> And froze the genial current of the ſoul.

Here are really two ideas. Penury, in the character of froſt, deprives the current of its heat, and checks its onward motion. I am unwilling to ſuppoſe the metaphor to be a broken one ; and that Gray jumbled into one, the images of horſemanſhip, and watery motion, as Addiſon has done in the following couplet ;

> I bridle in my ſtruggling muſe with pain,
> That longs to launch into a nobler ſtrain *.

* Letter from Italy.

XIV.

XIV.

Of the melancholy truth, that great parts are often kept from expanfion, by the influence of poverty and ignorance, the fourteenth Stanza feems to promife the illuftration, by reference made to analogous depreffions of excellence in the material and vegetable kingdoms. But more is promifed than performed. The examples are made up of fhewy images; but they are not examples in point. *Non erat his locus.*

The propofition to be illuftrated was, "that la-
" tent poffibilities of perfection, which favour-
" able fituations and circumftances might have
" *brought out*, are fometimes, by circumftances
" of an untowardly kind, prevented from being
" duly unfolded." Of this pofition illuftrations might eafily have been found, had not Gray confounded it with another, equally true with the former, yet altogether diftinct. That other pofition is, " that of perfections *already*
" *unfolded*, there may occur extrinfic caufes to
" prevent the beneficial difplay."

F

It

It is of this latter pofition, that Gray has
given the illuftration, in the images of " the
" *gem*, whofe brightnefs is hid by its depth in
" the fea ;" and of " the *flower*, whofe beauty
" and fragrance are loft, on account of the
" defert in which it grows." It is nothing to the
illuftration of the *former* pofition, that the flower
blufhes unfeen ; or that the gem may grow
where no hand can reach it. Had the
brightnefs of the gem remained folded up in
the *cruft*; or the flower been froft-nipt in the
bud, the images had been in point.

Of the images themfelves I have already allowed the merit. They are both, however, to
be found in Thomfon, from whom Gray feems
to have borrowed more than he thought fit
to acknowledge. Speaking of the influence of
the Sun, and univerfal operation of light ; he
fays *, in the way of addrefs to the operator,

> The unfruitful rock itfelf, impregn'd by thee,
> *In dark retirement* forms the lucid ftone.
> The lively diamond drinks thy *pureft rays*;
> Collected light compact.

And, defcribing the retirement of a rural
beauty †,

> As, in the hollow breaft of Apennine,
> Beneath the fhelter of encircling hills,

* Summer.   † Autumn.

A myrtle

A myrtle rifes, *far from human eye,*
And breathes its balmy fragrance o'er the wild;
So flourifh'd, *blooming, and, unfeen* by all,
The *fweet* Lavinia.

In the former example, the " diamond" of
Thomfon becomes the " gem" of Gray ; both
are *formed in retirement*; though Gray has changed the place; and tranfplanted the diamond
into the fea, for caufes that do not appear, and
with a propriety of which Criticifm entertains
a doubt. Both ftones are of " pureft ray."

Of the latter image, the identity is ftill more
obvious ; although it has been difguifed by the
change of a myrtle into a flower; and, perhaps, by a fhifting of the fcene from Italy to
Arabia Deferta. Why a flower was thought
better than a myrtle ; or a defert more proper
than a *fhelter'd* wafte, for rearing a tender plant,
we are not informed. To fee the fenfe of juftice return, is pleafant even when the return
is *late.* Gray, towards the end of his life,
dived to the bottom for the gem ; and, having brought it up, replanted it in the earth,
to be brought forth as occafion might call.
To the myrtle he made more fignal amends,
for its long transformation into a flower, by
making intereft with the Chancellor of the Uni-
verfity of Cambridge to have it created a bifhop.

Thy

Thy liberal heart, thy judging eye,
The *flower* unheeded fhall defcry,
And bid it round Heaven's altar fhed,
The fragrance of its blufhing head;
Shall raife from earth the latent *gem*,
To glitter on the diadem *.

Thomfon's myrtle " breathes its balmy fragrance o'er the wild;" Gray's flower " waftes
its fweetnefs on the defert air." " Waftes," in
place of " breathes," is an improvement;
though, whether *one* air is more " defert" than
another, the authority of Shakefpeare himfelf
will not hinder us to doubt.

It is often entertaining to trace imitation.
To deteƈt the adopted image, the copied defign, the transferred fentiment, the appropriated phrafe, and even the acquired manner and
frame, under all the difguifes that mutilation,
combination, and accommodation may have
thrown around them, muft require both parts
and diligence; but it will bring with it no ordinary gratification. A book, profeffedly on the
" Hiftory and progrefs of imitation in poetry,"
written by a man of perfpicacity, and an adept
in the art of difcerning likeneffes, even when
minute; with examples properly feleƈted, and
gradations duly marked; would make an im-
portant acceffion to the ftore of human literature, and furnifh rational curiofity with an
high regale.

* Inftallation Ode.

I remem-

I remember to have once heard, I know not where, or from whom, that Swift had projected a work of this kind. But Swift was full of projects; and scarcely possessed steadiness or industry sufficient to carry such a design through. I should have had better hopes of its success in the hands of Addison than of Swift. But I return to Gray.

To the *expression* in some parts of this Stanza, certain objections have been proposed. The word " bear," is thought to be improperly used, and to have been produced by the exigencies of the rhyme : " the caves of ocean *supporting* the precious stones that are formed there," is said to be an idea inept and insignificant. To this it has been urged in reply, that " bear," in this passage means " produce," in analogy to vegetable birth. But I am not sure that the analogy is not rather to animal production. Thus Waller, in a similar case, speaking of the sea :

——— 'tis so rockless and so clear,
That the rich bottom does appear
Pav'd all with precious things, not torn
From shipwreck'd vessels, *but there born* *.

And of the application of " born" to the flower itself, the same may be the account. It is not metaphysically used to denote necessity or fate; but physically to denote production. The use

* Loving at first-sight.

of " born" for " deftined," is too proverbial for poetry.

" Pureft ray ferene," has been cenfured by fome as obfcure, and by others as redundant. But that an expreſſion, which feems to have been ſtudiouſly *fought*, fhould have had no meaning in the mind of its author, it is fcarcely reaſonable to fuppofe. Gray, in the maturer part of his life, addicted himfelf to the ſtudy of natural hiſtory. It is not impoſſible that, in fome of the writers he had read on thefe ſubjects, he had found " ray ferene ;" [*raggio fereno* ;] ufed, as a technical term, for what, in precious ſtones, is commonly called the *water*.

" Pureft ray," taken by itfelf, is the expreſſion of Thomfon ; who afterwards calls it " collected light compact," according to a mode, not uncommon with him, of thruſting in his noun betwixt two *fhouldering* epithets ; in the ufe of which mode, he and his fellow imitators were, as I have heard Savage hu- moroufly obferve, *kept in countenance* by Mil- ton's " human face divine †."

Of this Stanza before I conclude the exa- mination, I am willing to gratify the Reader with a communication on the fubject, made me by the late Dr. Calvert Blake, a gentleman of eminent taſte, and moſt extenfive acquaint-

† Paradife Loſt, Book iii.

ance

ance with the body of English poetry; and who, by the cabals of trusted Malignity, was driven from high hopes of merited preferment; and forced, through a series of accumulating misfortunes (of the greatest part of which, as he informed me, he had a regular presentiment), to seek refuge in the mountains of Wales, where he taught the private school founded by the benefaction of the late Colonel Perkins, till death put an end to his distress.

It was the opinion of Dr. Blake, that Gray was drawn into this expression incidentally, by the instinctive operation of his ear, presenting him with indistinct and faint renewals of sounds which he had treasured up mechanically, and without purpose of recal. Thomson had said, "purest ray," and Milton, with an arrangement very like the present, "so thick a drop serene ‡;" and from the two together was formed by Gray his "purest ray serene." Thus far Dr. Blake. Whether his conjecture be well founded, I do not here mean to inquire. The coincidence of rhythm and form is remarkable. "Drop serene," is a translation of "gutta serena," a technical expression for a disease of the eyes, proceeding from an inspissation of humours, and terminating in the loss of sight. Of the application of the term *serene*, to a case where there is a total shutting out of light, Physic may be left at her own leisure to give her account.

‡ Paradise Lost, Book iii.

XV.

XV.

Of the fifteenth Stanza I find little to praife either in the Poetry or Politicks: for politicks it does contain; although it is part of a meditation on Death. Gray had paffed his youth like moft young men, who are taught, or teach themfelves, to confider fomething peculiarly refpectable as affociated with the character of *Whig*. Of the ebullitions of his uninformed youth, he was unfortunate enough to referve confiderable part for the plague of his riper age. Of his whiggifh prejudices his poetry is full.

That whiggifm is the beft *poetical* fide of the queftion, Candour is content to allow. If it feldom puts much money into the Poet's purfe, or brings with it much quiet to his mind, it is ufeful to him in the way of his profeffion; and when he works himfelf up to faction, he may be faid to " labour in his vocation." Of Liberty, the idea is fo vague, and the dimenfion fo little fettled, that the Poet may make of it what he will. The fairy land is all his own; and, however fantaftic his combinations may be, he will not want for fantaftic hearers to liften to his tale.

5   He

He may transform his Mortal into a "Goddefs" at will. He may chufe out for her what
proportions, and inveft her with what attributes
he chufes. He may array her in robes that
are "heavenly bright." He may describe
her as offering "Blifs" with profufion, and ready
to be delivered of "Delight:" "Pleafure" walk-
ing, crowned, with her arm in arm; and "Plenty,"
dreft in fmiles, bearing up her train behind;
whilft fhe fcatters her gifts on every fide; giving to Nature gaiety, to the Sun beauty, and
to the Day pleafure †. When he has thus finifhed off his goddefs, he may think of introducing her into company; and, whatever be the
fate of her gentleman ufher, the *Goddefs* is fure
of being well received by thofe that know the
value of fuch a vifitant.

Whatever may in general be urged or admit-
ted on the one fide or the other, concerning liberty, Criticifm muft be allowed, with pertinacity, to maintain, that the political creed of
Thomas Gray had nothing to do in the Elegy
written in a Country Church-yard. Not only is
this infertion out of place; it is alfo *ill-timed*.
The zealots of rebellion are no longer heroes in
Britain; and the appeal to the admiration of
the Reader, is toffed back in the Author's face.
Other times have brought with them other
principles. *Tempora mutantur & nos*—. The
fubtle diftinction, and inflammatory reafonings,

† Addifon. Letter from Italy.

G   that

that countenanced the fhedding of fanctified
blood, are no longer allowed a hearing. Even
the whiggifh Addifon has declared fuch reafonings to be *profanation*; pronouncing, almoft
a century ago, and of his own favoured Milton, that

—— *Now* the language can't fupport the caufe *.

Of diftinguifhed models of human excellence
—of characters high-finifhed, both in under-
ftanding and heart, there is no want, either in
the general hiftory of mankind, or in the particular hiftory of this ifland : and Aftonifhment
cannot help doubling her ufual portion of wonder, that from among the affembled worthies
of the world, Gray could find none deferving
felection, as patterns of greatnefs to Man, fave
three defperate partizans of faction, and pro-
moters of a rebellion, that fubverted both the
laws and government of his country.

Of thefe three characters, only one is held
up to any cenfure. Even on him the cenfure
is made to fall obliquely, and after it has had
its force broken by a whiggifh arm. The cenfure itfelf too is of whiggifh make. Of Cromwell, the crime is declared to have been the
fhedding his *country*'s blood. For his *King*'s,
Gray returns " *ignoramus* " on the bill.

* Account of the greateft Englifh Poets.

XVI.

XVI.

In the fixteenth Stanza is contained more, in the way of allufion to thefe heroes and their tranfactions; but allufion, at which Criticifm finds herfelf obliged to ftop fhort. Though the evil temper of the times *did* enable them to " command the applaufe of liftening fenates," which is poetical language, for being *well heard in the Houfe*; yet, with what propriety, can any of them be faid to have " fcatter'd plenty o'er a fmiling land ?" Of a land that has its plough-fhare turned into a fword, the plenty is not great: nor was England dreft in fmiles in the time of the great rebellion.

In this Stanza too, Gray is guilty of an inconfiftency. " To defpife the threats of pain and ruin," is not of the clafs of virtues that the poor man's lot forbids, even according to the views of Gray. On his " village Hamden," notwithftanding the meannefs of his lot, he forgets that, in the former Stanza, he conferred a *dauntlefs breaft*, in all the forms of inveftiture. But the difgrace of this inconfiftency is due to him, for having, on an occafion like this, fuffered his mind to be bewildered with politicks. It is a great blot upon the piece. Of a work, fuch as this, the fenti-

ments

ments ought to be fuch as every heart will return; the appeals, fuch as every mind will admit. Death generalifes the fpecifications of political tenets. The Grave takes in all parties. There is no Shibboleth among her fubjects.

The "reading their hiftory in a nation's eyes," is a thought that holds more of Rhetorick than Poetry. "Hiftory" is too indefinite a term. There is good hiftory, and there is bad. It is no exclufive privilege of the *good*, to be able to read their hiftory thus. The *bad* come in for their fhare. Nor do the *rich* enjoy here any power of appropriation, which extends not alfo to the *poor*, in degree. The *expreffion* is a forced one. We commonly read the hiftories of *others :* feldom *our own*.

XVII. XVIII.

Of the two following Stanzas, the *compofition* is faulty in refpect to their connection with the preceding, and with each other. Even where the compofition is in couplets, the faftidious critic is unwilling that the fenfe fhould be made out by the couplets' bearing in upon each other. When the Stanza exceeds two lines in number, the effect is yet more difagreeable.

able. The plea of neceſſity is urged with leſs reaſon; and the contraſt betwixt the completed circumſcription of found, and the yet uncompleted accumulation of ſenſe, becomes more revolting, as it becomes more felt.

With this blemiſh, the Stanzas under conſideration are chargeable. Gray was not unapprized of it; and, that it might be leſs perceptible as a blemiſh, he gave orders, in the firſt edition, that no diſtinction of Stanzas ſhould be marked *. In a *Scotch edition*, however, of his Poems, which he ſeems to have thought likely to extend his fame, the natural diſtinction of Stanzas is reſtored, as it is in many others, particularly in Mr. Maſon's. The device was but a ſhallow one, and very properly relinquiſhed. In verſe of this alternate ſtructure, the lines *form themſelves* into quaternions: and the bringing out theſe quaternions ſeparately to the eye, is only a technical contrivance, enabling us to parcel them more readily. Inſtead of attempting to conceal the fault, Gray ſhould have tried to mend it.

In the *ſenſe* I find little to blame, that may not be referred to ſome of the former ſtrictures on this Elegy. "Virtues," and "crimes," are ideas too particular for the Author's view in this place, which is meant to extend to the circumſcription, from cauſes extrinſic, of the range of *natural*, as well as *moral*, action.

* Maſon.

"Hiding

" Hiding the ftruggling pangs of confcious truth," and " quenching the blufhes of inge- nuous fhame," are only different defcriptions of the fame action, viz. the " checking the dictates of confcience." " Quenching blufhes," is an idea fcarcely correct; though by the quench- ing of *heat*, blufhes may be made to dif- appear. That the poor man's lot forbids the bearing down the fuggeftions of confcience, is only *relatively* true. Profligacy is free of all corporations.

XIX.

In the nineteenth Stanza is defcribed, in a manner that is pleafing, the calm and content- ed ftate of an unafpiring and meek mind. But what defcription can there be, in which fuch a picture will not pleafe ? The two firft lines are, from the arrangement, equivocal : but we know what the Author ought to mean. It is not, that " their wifhes never ftrayed far from the ftrife of the crowd ;" but that, " naturally retired from that ftrife, they formed no wifh to ftray from fuch retirement." Yet the words " crowd," and " ignoble," are not hap- pily felected, to be brought forward in a defcription

fcription of the contentions of the " mighty,"
and the " great." The two clofing lines have
in them fomething of foftnefs, that makes
Criticifm deal cenfure with reluctance :

> Along the cool, fequeftered vale of life,
> They kept the noifelefs tenor of their way.

Yet even here, the idea, as ufual, is prefented
to us in different afpects. Ambition is painted
as a *hot*, and then as a *noify*, perfonage ; and
to thefe views of his character are oppofed the
" cool vale," and the " noifelefs tenor," that
are thought fit to be affociated with the character of the Man of Content. Gray never
could be brought to fee when he had faid
enough.

XX. XXI. XXII. XXIII.

The four Stanzas that follow, are to me the
moft pleafing in the Elegy. The notions appear to Memory, original; though to Belief and
Feeling, imitations. But, great as is their general merit, in fome particulars they are faulty.
The facrednefs of the Critic's truft, impofes on
him fometimes the exertion of felf-denial ;
obliging him to range for blemifhes, where
his wifhes are to find nought but beauties.

In

" In the firft of the four, the expreffion " thefe bones," where only *perfons* had been fpoken of, is awkward. " Their bones," would have been lefs exceptionable. To " protect from infult," is profaic; and, if the end of the " memorial" was this protection, there is no neceffity that we be put in mind, by the fuggeftion of the *frailnefs* of that memorial, that the end will not be anfwered. A *memorial*, protecting from *infult*, is a mode of expreffion approaching to nonfenfe. If protection be ever the refult of its erection, it is only in a fecondary way.

The twenty-firft Stanza does not fet out happily. " Their name," their years :" whofe name ? whofe years ? They were bones, not perfons, that were mentioned : and a nomenclature of bones, followed with the age of each, engraved over their refpective repofitories, is too ludicrous a fancy to be allowed place in the judgment for a moment. Of the meaning there is no doubt; but of that meaning, the expreffion is unlucky. In all compofitions that are ferious, the remoteft temptation to what is ludicrous fhould be refifted. Of this idea, Gray himfelf feems to have felt the truth, and has alluded to it forcibly in his fhort ftrictures on * Sterne's Sermons, " They are juft," fays he, " what fermons fhould be : but the " Preacher often totters on the verge of rifi-

* Mafon.

bility,

" bility, and feems ready to *dafh his periwig* in
" the faces of his auditors." Sterne's rifibility
was buffoonery; and an outrage to tafte as well
as decency. With this Gray is not chargeable.
But in a cafe where much caution is neceffary,
it is not enough not to have erred with inten-
tion. The writer is bound to be *watchful*. For
even in the funeral proceffion levity is fometimes feen to mix; and ftands perked up in
the corner of the aile, with the grin already
lined on his face, and prepared to come out
full in a moment, if but the flighteft down
from the plumage of the hearfe, born towards
him by the gentleft breath, fhould chance to
tickle his cheek. *Hunc tu Romane caveto.*

" The unlettered mufe fpelling out the
" names of the rufticks upon their tomb-
" ftones;" is a good image. It has in it more
alfo of *life* than Parnell's idea:

The flat fmooth ftones that bear a name,
The chiffel's flender help to fame.

The " ftrewing of the holy texts" too is gra-
phical.

That fome *fchooling* is neceffary to induce re-
fignation to death, the general pofition is juft;
though not requiring the quantity of dilatation
he has given it in the two following ftanzas.
Of the word "Moralift," the application is falfe
and provincial. A Moralift is " one who
" *teaches* the duties of life." It is the unlet-

H   tered

tered Mufe that is the moralift, not the ruftic ;
who only *takes* the leffon which his teacher of-
fers to give. Should we even ftretch the com-
pafs of the word, fo as to make it comprehend
both the teacher and the taught, the term
would be ftill improper in this place. The
leffons are not in morality, but religion. They
are not arguments, but authorities. I do not
know that the verfe would have fuffered much,
either in ftrength or beauty, had the Author's
piety perfuaded him to prefent it thus :

That teach the ruftic *Chriftian* to die.

Gray had too much devotion about him to be
afhamed of the word Chriftian. His obfervations on Lord Shaftefbury's character and
writings fhow that he was himfelf a Chriftian,
although a polite man ; and that he had fenfe
enough to fee, and fpirit enough to defpife, the
duplicity and cowardice of him, who rears up
morality into a mole, which he may make ufe
of in battering revelation.

Should Criticifm be afked, what blemifh fhe
has difcovered in the two ftanzas that follow :
" For who to dumb forgetfulnefs, &c." fhe
has this general objection to propofe againft
them, that they are too *diffufive*. The thought
has been already ftated. Of that thought they
are meant to be illuftrative. But the illuftration is too long. Of correct writing, it is one

A   of

of the eſſential laws not to ſwell out the com-
ment ſo as to become more momentous than
the text. The acceſſories are proper in their
own place : but to joſtle out the principal,
they ſhould never be allowed.

What the firſt of theſe two ſtanzas chiefly
holds out to Cenſure, is its *expreſſion*. It is not
clear in what view "Forgetfulneſs" is pronounced
" dumb." That what is not remembered will,
of courſe, not be uttered, is a truth; but of
denominatives the ſelection is better made, by
reference to the internal nature of the object,
than to circumſtances only conſequential.
" Warm precincts" has been cenſured; and
" precincts of day." Yet " *luminis oras*" is
ſaid by Virgil; and " *aridos fines Libyæ*" by
more writers than I can name. " Precinct" is
ſynonymous with " *ora*" and " *fines*;" and ſig-
nifies not the " outline" only, but alſo the
" encloſed ſpace." In this laſt ſenſe, with the
accent differently placed, it is uſed by Milton * :

Through all reſtraint broke looſe, he wings his way
Not far off heaven, *in the precincts of light*,
Directly towards the new-created world,

That Gray, moving, himſelf, in the *precincts
of light*; and within the pale of an univerſity
claiming to herſelf a *monopoly* of that, and other

* Paradiſe Loſt, iii. 87.

H 2   ſciences;

fciences ; fhould have fo far unlearned the philofophy of light, as to fuppofe that the man
who is placed in a region where light exilts not,
may take up the objects of fight, is matter of
fome furprife. He that has already left the
precincts of day, will caft no " lingering look"
either *behind* or *before :* he has no look to caft.
Vifibility and illumination reciprocate; and
from a place to which the rays of the object
extend not, the object is not feen.

Of " longing lingering look," the con-
ftruction, in refpect to found, is in his ufual
ftyle. " High-born Hoel's harp." " * Light
Llewellyn's lay." What is acquired to the
defcription by the three *l*'s in " longing lingering look," it is not eafy to fee. But Criticifm is willing to check the feverity of cenfure for a fault, which *Criticks* have in a great
meafure caufed. The flack and folemn dictates that have paffed from mouth to mouth
upon the fubject of reprefentative poetry, from
the days of Homer to thofe of his tranflator
Pope, have mifled men of greater tafte and
judgment than Gray. On this occafion, however, he feems to have forgot his *accidence* ; and
miftaken what his mafters taught. Liquids,
according to the doctrines of the reprefentative
fchool, are imitative of *accelerated* motion. Of

* Soft.

thefe

thefe doctrines, in the prefent cafe, he has made but a froward application, when he makes his liquids reprefentative of the motion of the laggard paffengers that *hang back* in their way to death.

Of all the elementary conftituents of oral articulate found, there is no one which has had more attention paid to it by the adepts in re-prefentative compofition, than the femi-vocal incompofite *l.* It is eafy of accefs, ready to grant, or even proffer its fervices; and ever within call. To it, of all the reft, Gray feems to have paid peculiar court. The kindnefs of Dr. Curzon, late of Brazen Nose, and now refiding in Italy for his health, and to whom I embrace this opportunity of recording my obligation for materials that have been of ufe to me in the prefent work, has put me in pof-feffion of a little relic of Gray, furnifhing a ftriking illuftration of his fondnefs for this let-ter, and how much, as the Doctor terms it, it had infenfibly *gained his ear.* Of this relic I do not know that, in any edition of Gray's works, the communication has yet been indulg-ed the Public; not even in that one in which the Author's literary correfpondence, and frag-ments of projected poems; have been printed. I am contented, therefore, to give it to the world, with part of the letter into which it was

copied,

copied, as particularly connected with the prefent fubject, and as illuftrative moreover of that
leading feature in the character of Gray, *the
love of project*; hoping that I may do it without offence; as, in offering this gratification
to rational literary curiofity, for which I have
the Doctor's permiffion, I invade no property,
nor violate any known right.

Of this piece the fubject, when mentioned,
will convince thofe that write for the information of mankind at large, what danger attends
the enunciation of univerfal propofitions; and
how much credit with the Public thofe have
rifked, who have taken upon them to maintain
with pertinacity, that at no period of his poetical life Gray ever wrote verfes on *love*. It is
a little piece, fomewhat of the *Namby Pamby*
kind; wrought out in the manner of a fong,
and compofed (if one may judge, from internal
marks, of writings whofe dates are purpofedly
concealed) at the particular time of his life at
which his enthufiafm for Italian poetry and
Italian mufic raged moft. He calls it a
POETICAL RONDEAU; a title which probably he would have altered afterwards, had he
thought the piece worth claiming. Of the
nature of the project (for fo he modeftly enough
calls it), together with the view which gave
rife to it, he gives the following account; at

once

once tending to fhew it to be fomewhat fingular, and proving the folly of him who, in
this *aged* ftate of literary communication, fhall
fay to himfelf, " Go to; I fhall fit down, and
" write me fomething new."

" I have often wondered," fays he, " that
" the analogies of thefe fifter Arts (he had been
" fpeaking of Poetry and Mufic) have not
" been more keenly traced out and marked,
" with a view to mutual transference. Each
" has many things in her budget, which fhe
" might give out occafionally in loan to the
" other, without inconvenience to herfelf.
" Mufic, for inftance, who is the more fprightly
" of the two, and moreover the younger and
" handfomer—(but let that be under the rofe);
" —having had a great many different lovers,
" fome of them far travelled, and very *ton*-ifh
" of courfe, has picked up, during the time
" they have danced after her, a world of little
" curiofities and trinkets, as well as things of
" more ferious ufe, in the way of drefs, orna-
" ment, &c. with all which fhe occafionally
" tricks herfelf off, and makes in them, I affure
" you, *a charming fweet figure*; fhe has alfo had
" now and then a *penfive* lover: but from them
" fhe has borrowed little elfe than ferious man-
" ner; which fhe very quickly puts off again, left,
" as fhe fays, it fpoil her flow of fpirits. So
" much

" much for Mifs Mufic. Now for her fifter;
" with whom you muft know I am a lit-
" tle acquainted. She again is of a more
" fteady deportment : keeps her looks very
" well : has no averfion to a frolic now and
" then : but then it muft be with thofe fhe is
" well acquainted with; for fhe is more referv-
" ed than her fifter, and fets up more on fenfe
" than fprightlinefs. She too has had fome
" lovers.; though fhe does not give them much
" encouragement, confidering them in general
" as danglers; but of the few whom fhe efteem-
" ed and thought fhe could truft, fhe has not
" difdained now and then to accept fomething
" in the way of remembrance, and even to wear
" it occafionally for their fake. Now what I
" would have thefe two ladies do is this. I
" would have each of them empty her drawers
" and band-boxes, throw all the things together,
" and turn the two wardrobes into one. By this
" means, as I told them, the *things* of each would
" in effect be doubled; for the world is not to
" know. To this fcheme the younger, who thought
" it a fine frolic, very readily agreed. The elder
" has afked time to think of it; and in the
" mean time has got, at my inftigation, a mil-
" liner engaged to look over her fifter's things,
" and fee which will fit her beft. By par-
" ticular defire alfo of your humble fervant,
" (nay

" (nay don't look wife, for " 'pon 'onnor"
" she *won't have me*) she is to make her first ex-
" periment to-morrow, and come down to tea
" in a trim airy drefs of her fifter's, which I
" always liked on Mifs Mufic, and. which, I
" pledged my tafte, would become *her* too.

" *Quo te Mæri pedes ?* you fay---well, as you
" have been civil, and have put up your *Mæri*
" in your pocket, which I grant you might have
" flung at me, though *mark*, the quantity would
" have been *too much*,—I fay, as you have dealt
" by me like a *civil gentleman*, I am going to
" come down from my flights, and tell you
" shortly what I mean. *Summa fequar faftigia*
" *rerum.*——A long and unintermitted enthu-
" fiafm for mufic has, you know, led, *volven-*
" *tibus annis*, to the difcovery of many varied
" modes of mufical expreffion ; and introduced
" multiplied conveyances of mufical pleafure.
" There are many of thefe which I think might
" be transferred to the fifter art Poetry with
" fuccefs. The enclofed, which you no doubt
" read before the letter, and I hope have done
" me the honour to think the ferious effufion
" of a *non-erubefcend* flame—(by the way, the
" word is not yet Englifh I believe*),—contains
" an Effay Piece in the way of this fcheme.
" The fame is entitled a *Poetical Rondeau.* Nay,

* There is as yet no fuch Englifh word. The word *non-*
defcript, lately introduced, upon a fimilar analogy, is not
lefs ridiculous.

* I   " do

" do not ſtare. Be ſure the ſtranger prove no
" old acquaintance, before you thruſt him from
" your chambers, and ſhut the door in his face.
" You know the principle of the *Rondeau* in
" muſic. It is " to give a ſubject *eaſe* by the
" familiarity ariſing from repetition, and *intereſt*
" by diverſification." What is known, alter-
" nates with what is unknown. They mutu-
" ally lead in each other: and give to each
" other a mutual RELIEF. The little trifle I
" ſent you encloſed, is an attempt at this al-
" ternation, *in Poetry.* Accordingly, when you
" have firſt duly armed yourſelf with your
" double concaves, you ſhall ſee, in the piece
" before you, firſt of all, come in—the SUB-
" JECT; which is afterwards to come in, as the
" RETURN. This Subject you ſhall ſee to
" be taken from the department of *Love*;
" viz. " the pain of parting;" which B-tt-e,
" if you find him in the mood, will pour away
" to you with his uſual ſenſibility, in a different
" ſhape, in the character of Polly Peachum.—
" Well then, the *Subject* drawing to a cloſe, you
" ſhall ſee us nick the time, and *prepare* the
" laſt cadence, ſo as to *lead in* what ſeems to
" be a *new* ſubject, but is nothing but a modi-
" fication of the *old;*—this is the *firſt departure*;
" which muſt be ſo managed as to preſerve at
" the cloſe of it a ready lead in to the *return,*
" —which now makes its appearance again,—

2   " ſhews

" which muſt be ſo managed as to preſerve at
" the cloſe of it a ready lead in to the *return,*
" ---which now makes its appearance again,---
" ſhews itſelf away a little,---and then---leads
" off to the *ſecond departure. This* muſt be, at
" once, a diverſiſication of the *Subject,* and of the
" *firſt departure;*---it may contain a more *labour-*
" *ed* air, and greater changes of key, or, &c.---
" we muſt not however keep long upon it: for
" lo! cometh the Return again;---then lead we
" off to the *third* departure, with a very *learned*
" modulation, plying in ſo at the end however,
" as to admit the Return, a *fourth* time.---Now
" for the great trial of ſkill, in leading off
" to the *laſt* departure, which is to be a *minore ;*
" and muſt, if it is to be worth a farthing, be
" connected; at the expence of ſome pains,
" with the cloſing cadence of the Return that
" precedes it.---Then warble away at the *minore*
" itſelf; which muſt repay the favour, and
" make way courteouſly for the ſaid Return ;
" which now comes in, once more, to claim
" her firſt occupancy, and remain miſtreſs of
" the premiſes.——Thus far Theory,---now
" enter Practice."

POETICAL

POETICAL RONDEAU.

First to love,—and then to part,—
Long to seek a mutual heart,—
Late to find it :—and, again,
Leave, and lose it—oh the pain !

    Some have loved, and loved (they say)
    'Till they loved their love away ;
    Then have *left* ; to love anew :
    But, I wot, they loved not *true !*

True to love,—and then to part,—
Long to seek a mutual heart,—
Late to find it,—and, again,
Leave, and lose it—oh the pain !

    Some have lov'd, to pass the time ;
    And have lov'd their love in rhyme :
    Loath'd the love ; and loath'd the song :
    But their love could not be *strong !*

Strong to love,—and then to part,
Long to seek a mutual heart,—
Late to find it—and, again,
Leave and lose it,—oh the pain !

    They who just but felt the flame,
    Lightly lambent o'er their frame,—
    Light to them the parting knell :
    For, too sure, they love not *well !*

Well to love,—and then to part,—
Long to seek a mutual heart,—
Late to find it,—and, again,
Leave, and lose it,—oh ! the pain !

    But when once the potent dart,
    Cent'ring, rivets heart to heart,
    Then to sever what is bound,
    Is to tear the closing wound.

Thus to love,—and then to part,—
Long to seek a mutual heart,—
Late to find it,—and, again,
Leave, and lose it,—oh ! the pain ! . . . .

" *Nous voilà*---and now for my friend Bentley
" to do me off nicely the *device* ; being two
" faithful

" faithful hearts, that shall seem both *two* and
" *one*; so closely are they hasped together with
" a true love dart : the *barb* holding fast the
" one, and the " grey goose wing that is there-
" on" the other ;---take notice though---the
" *other* is the *female* heart; and take notice of
" the emblem too. It is only kept on by the
" *feather*. A little matter will make it slip off."

Thus far the letter and its illustration. To
him who is not an adept in any art, it is a matter of difficulty to ascertain whether he has
apprehended aright the import of the technical terms and phrases used in the language of
that art. But if I have attained a proper conception of what is aimed at in the *levity* how
inserted, the idea itself is not so novel, as the
manner of stating it seems to make it. Of
the ancient Dithyrambick Odes, whose chief
excellence seems to have been their obscurity
and affectation (qualities in which they might
find many of the modern lyrical compositions
qualified to vie with them), a particular species
were denominated *Cyclic*, or circular. These
circular Odes probably proceeded on the principle
of Gray's Poetical Rondeau; as did also certain
of the more sprightly and convivial songs or
glees ; such for example as that one of Anacreon, of which the return or burthen is

’Οτ’ ἐγω πιω τον οινον.———

As to the levity itself, I think I may say
with truth, that its composition must have cost
more

more labour than it is ever likely to pay. It
holds of the Italian fchool : has in it more of
found than fenfe : and the little fenfe it has, is
not much helped forward by the found; notwithftanding the accelerating power of the letter *l*, which he has here ufed upon the principles of his mafters, although with too much
profufion, and fcarcely with any fuccefs.—
Enough of the letter *l*; reprefentative poetry;
and poetical Rondeaus.

XXIII.

In the twenty-third Stanza, the laft of the
four formerly mentioned, is held out a fentiment
which Criticifm is willing to praife, till, col-
lecting her ideas, fhe remembers having beftow-
ed praife on its contrary. Does the " fome
fond breaft," do the " fome pious drops," alluded to, contribute to take from the bitter-
nefs of death, and fmooth the paffage to the
world of fpirits ? So fays Gray. But what fays
Parnel *, in a cafe pretty fimilar ? *Audi alteram
partem :*

* Night-Piece.

Nor

Nor can the parted body know,
Nor needs the foul thefe forms of woe.

And Thomfon * :

—— How many ftand
Around the death-bed of their deareft friends,
And *point the parting anguifh!*

Sterne too, whofe diffipation was too fhort-
lived, completely to deftroy in him the feeds
of fenfibility and nature, has defcribed, in a
Book of which about one-fifth part is worth
reading, the fympathies of furrounding friends,
as conftituting the acuteft part of a dying man's anguifh.   Having recorded his
wifh to die in an inn (a fpecies of death for
which there are few competitors), he proceeds
thus : " At home,—I know it,—the concern
" of my friends, and the laft fervices of wiping
" my brow, and fmoothing my pillow, which
" the quivering hand of pale Affection fhall pay .
" me, will fo *crucify my foul,* that I fhall die
" of a diftemper which my phyfician is not
" aware of."

Amongft Doctors who thus difagree, who
fhall fettle the difpute ?   To a mind given to
fhift its views, and to Senfibilities not yet properly *made up,* both afpects of the fact, and both
impreffions of the fentiment, offer themfelves

* Winter.

in

in turn; and both are in turn approved. Of this *viciffitude* of feeling, no man is without his fhare. As the frame of the mind alters, fo alter its likings, and its prepoffeffion in favour of a fentiment, or its oppofite. Of fentiments *exclufively* juft, the catalogue would be but fmall. *Relative* truth is all we have a title to expect in the department of Tafte; of which, as no ftandard exifts, it is vain to fuppofe any ftandard fhould be found. Scepticifm, dangerous in philofophy, and impious in religion, urges a reafonable plea for admiffion into the Court of Criticifm; of whofe decifions fhe may temper the feverity, and diminifh the felf-importance.

With thefe mutually contradictory fentiments (to which the late Mr. Savage gave the name of *ambidextrous* *, and of which he had made large collections from the body of Englifh Poetry that then exifted), to which the mind makes alternate love, as the Antiquary beftows his ad-

---

* The appropriation of the word is contrary to analogy. *Colliding* would have been more proper. On the occafions alluded to, it is the *mind* that is ambidextrous; not the *fentiments*. Savage, whofe fancy led him to form more projects than his fituation allowed him to execute, feems to have intended fome work upon this fubject. But to render the defign complete, his Collections, of which I retain an indiftinct idea, fhould have taken in profe-writers as well as poets, and other languages as well as the Englifh.

miration,

miration, now on the *image* of the medal, and
now on the *reverfe*, the writings of all authors
of fancy are replete: We recognife them, at
times contradicting each other, and at times
contradicting themfelves. The language of the
Leafowes is, that to the paffionate lover, the
wonted haunts of the beloved object give gratification, when from thefe haunts fhe is abfent.

> They tell me, my favourite maid,
> The pride of that valley, is gone :
> Alas ! *where with her I have ftrayed,*
> *I could wander with pleafure alone* *.

The image is one that pleafes for the time : but
reflected from the lakes of Hagley, which is
only a few miles off, it meets the eye with its
form inverted; and yet it pleafes ftill.

> The fhades of Hagley now have loft their boaft.—
> How, in the world, to me a defert grown,
> Abandoned and alone,
> Without my fweet companion, can I live ! †

There are frames of mind that fuit either view.
It is not in Poetry as in Logic. Here two con-
tradictories may dwell together, each of equal
authority with its oppofite.

Though Poetry may be juftifiable in prefenting us with oppofite views, each of which *may*
be true for the time, yet fhe ought to beware,
when fhe is dealing out her *univerfals*, that fhe

---

* Shenftone. Abfence.   † Littleton. Monody.

K   offer

offer us not a *relative*, in place of an *abfolute*, truth. It is in this view that Gray is cenfurable in the prefent inftance. That the fympathies of friends give eafe to a dying man, may be, in general, as juft a fentiment as that they give him pain ; that they *foften* his anguifh, as that they *point* it : but here the enunciation is didactic. The Poet fpeaks in no character, and to no particular clafs, but brings forth the fentiment in the form of a *pofition* ; and confidered as a pofition, it is not true.

The third line of the Stanza contains an hyperbole, which is out-hyperboled in the fourth :

Even from the grave the voice of Nature cries :
Even in our afhes live their wonted fires.

a pofition at which Experience revolts, Credulity hefitates, and even Fancy ftares. He who can bring himfelf to believe, that he has heard the voice of Nature crying from the grave of a dead man, is *in train* to affent in time to the propofition, that " even in our afhes live their " wonted fires :" though Friendfhip fhould caution him to ftop fhort, and Pleafantry fuggeft to him that *furface* views are oft delufive ; and that he may find himfelf, on this occafion, if he goes farther on, *incedere per* IGNES *fuppofitos cinere* DOLOSO. But I am afhamed at the expenditure of precious time, incurred by the examination of a propofition contrary to all truth,

truth, abſtract or poetical; which Madneſs cannot ſhape itſelf to the conviction of, nor elon-
gations more that Pindaric bring Imagination
in contact with even for a moment.

What makes this conceit (if by the name
conceit may be called that which cannot be
conceived) the more unpardonable in Gray is,
that, (by a proceſs of judgment the reverſe of
that formerly commemorated, with regard to
the cloſing line of a ſtanza in his Ode on Spring)
he introduced the line in which it is conveyed
in place of another; and as an improvement
of the original thought †. The Stanza in its
firſt ſtate concluded with this line,

> Awake and faithful to her wonted fires.

which, if we chaſten ſtill farther, upon the
ſuggeſtion of Mr. Maſon, into

> Awake and faithful to her *firſt deſires*;

we ſhall then, inſtead of two hyperboles, have
only one, lengthened by the addition of a tail.
I think Maſon has informed us, that he adviſed
him to alter the line. But Gray could not
afford to want it; for here it is probable he
once intended to conclude the Elegy; and this
mode of " twirling off the thought into an
" apophthegm," he thought the moſt ſtriking
he could find.

† Maſon.

K 2   Gray

Gray has, in a note on this line, endeavoured to juftify the thought by a reference to a paffage in Petrarch. But no authority can give dignity to nonfenfe, or tranfmute falfe tafte into true. As to the writings of Petrarch, it may be allowed that in them, as in moft of the Italian poetry, many inftances of conceit occur. Yet more have been fancied than found. A Poet who poffeffes this vein in himfelf, imagines he meets with it wherever he goes. Thoughts apparelled in the fimpleft garb, appear to him dreft out in point. The ideas that pafs in review before him, partake of the colour of his mind; and his fancy, like Shakefpeare's green-eyed monfter, " *makes* the food " it feeds on." Ovid abounds in conceits and quaintneffes; but the eyes of Cowley multiplied them, as they did thofe of Petrarch, to infinity.

After reference thus foberly made to the authority of Petrarch, Curiofity will, no doubt, prick up his ears when he is told, that the paffage quoted from that Poet, contains not the fentiment in queftion. Mafon, whofe tafte was too good to make him admit the authority of Petrarch in defence of an unnatural thought, feems not however to have doubted that the thought was really his. And indeed if, of the fonnet referred to, the three lines quoted by Gray be taken detached from the reft, they may.

may, though fomewhat awkwardly, be made
to convey that thought. Taken along with the
context, and in connection with its defign, the
wildnefs of the idea vanifhes, and propriety
and nature inveft it.

The Poet is complaining of the hopeleffnefs
of his love *. " The flame I cherifh, fays he,
" how intenfe! yet how unrewarded! and even
" unperceived! unperceived by her whom I alone
" wifh to recognife it, though marked by all
" befides! Ah, diftruftful fair-one! in whom
" much beauty is mixed with little faith, look
" at my love-lorn eye, and doubt my paffion
" if you can.—No, you cannot, you do not
" doubt it; but my lucklefs ftar hardens your
" heart againft my ardent love. Yet not un-
" rewarded fhall be my paffion, although un-
" rewarded by you, The tuneful homage
" which you regard not, fhall gain me immor-
" tal fame. The flame which you repay not
" with kindred flame, fhall fpread its conta-
" gion over many hearts. As a living prin-
" ciple, it fhall pervade my verfe. I fee it in
" Fancy's eye, fhooting its fparks into future
" ages; and (when the two fair orbs that in-
" fpired it are fhut, and the tongue that fung
" their praifes is cold) fetting the world on
" fire."---Verfified thus:

* Petr. Son. 169.

Ah!

Ah ! how within me glows the fubtle flame !
To all but one fair infidel confefs'd.
She, only dear, fupreme in worth and fame,
She only, doubts her empire in my breaft :
Thou rich in beauty !—yet, in faith how poor !
Speaks not my fever'd eye the wafting grief ?
—But for my lucklefs ftar, ere now, full fure,
Some drops from Pity's fount had brought relief.

   Yet glows not, meedlefs quite, the warm defire ;
But, when our duft has filled the fatal urn,
   Long, in my verfe, fhall live the genial fire,
Which thy cold bofom warm'd to no return.
   Wide fhall its fparks the kindred flame infpire ;
And other Lauras melt ; — and other Petrarchs mourn.

So much for this celebrated fentiment in the Elegy written in a Country Church-yard, which it is herefy not to maintain, and fluggifhnefs not to feel : and fo much for the paffage of Petrarch, on which Gray fuppofed he had built it. If * one line, in which there is a little of *point*, be excepted, the fonnet of which it makes the clofe, is as fimple as ever was fung. A tuneful lover confoles himfelf for the hardnefs of his miftrefs's heart, by anticipating the enthufiafm with which pofterity will read the verfes in which he has fung her praife. Here is no voice of Nature crying from the grave of the dead ; here are no inurned afhes glowing with pofthumous fires. It is not the afhes of

* " Fredda *una* lingua, et *due* begli occhi chiufi."

Petrarch

Petrarch and Laura that glow, but posterity that glows when they are no more.

On this sonnet of Petrarch, misfortune seems to have been *entailed.* Cowley, to whom Petrarch was an inexhaustible mine, struck upon it in one of his days of digging. He knew it by its general appearance to be *ore*, and set himself accordingly to smelt it ; but so clumsily did he perform the operation, and so much heterogeneous metal did he suffer to run into it, that the most skilled assayers can scarcely know to what composition to refer it. It makes one of the pieces of *The Mistress*, and is here given to the Reader, both as being a curiosity in itself, and as illustrating that part of Cowley's poetical character, hinted in these strictures on Gray, and stated elsewhere at length.

HER UNBELIEF.

I.

'Tis a *strange kind* of unbelief in you,
That you your *vict'ries* should not spy :
Vict'ries *begotten* by your *eye.*——
That your bright beams, as those of comets do,
Should kill ; but not know *how*, or *who.*

II.

That, *truly*, you my *idol* may appear,
—Whilst all the people smell and see,
The od'rous flames I *offer* thee,
Thou sitt'st, and do'st not see, nor smell, nor hear,
Thy constant, zealous, *worshipper.*

III.

III.

They fee't too well, who at my fires repine,
Nay, th' *un*-concern'd themfelves do prove
Quick-ey'd enough to fpy'my love.
Nor does the *caufe* in thy face clearer fhine,
Than the *effect* appears in mine.

IV.

Fair infidel ! by what unjuft decree,
Muft *I*, who, with fuch reftlefs care,
Would make this truth to thee appear,—
Muft I, who *preach*, and *pray* for't, be
Damn'd, by thy *incredulity ?*

V.

I, by thy unbelief am, guiltlefs, flain.
O have but *faith*, and then, that you
That faith may know for to be *true*,
It fhall, itfelf b' a *miracle* maintain ;
And raife *me* from the *dead* again. — &c.

What an heterogeneous mafs is here ! what a
chaos of jarring elements ! *Frigida pugnantia
calidis, humentia ficcis.* This fad Miftrefs is,
firft, an *infidel*; then fhe is a *gainer of battles*;
which battles are *begot*; and their father is *her
eye.* That eye however is a *blind* one; as blind
as a *comet.* Then fhe becomes the *idol Baal*;
and is not only blind but *deaf*; and without the
fenfe of *fmelling :* but that does not hinder *her
face from fhining.* Next fhe is transformed into

6

Caufe ;

Caufe; and her lover into *Effect:* after which fhe
becomes an infidel again; and her lover is
transformed into a *prieft*; in which character
he both *preaches* and *prays*, to convert her;
but all to no purpofe: for, after having run
the rifk of *damnation*, he is actually put to
death: yet that does not damp his zeal. He
is refolved to make one trial more; and,
finding all other arguments fail, propofes
the great one of *miracles*; undertaking, if fhe
will firft believe *on truft*, to *rife*, himfelf, from
the dead, in order to *confirm her faith.*——
Such is the procefs in this piece; a procefs, in
the contemplation of which Reafon feels herfelf humbled; and Fancy, put to fhame;
whilft Religion reclaims indignant, that her
myfteries fhould fuffer profanation by fuch
abfurd and wanton allufions.

What now remains of the Elegy, partakes of
the nature of an After-piece. In his " Elegy
" to the Memory of an Unfortunate Lady,"
the vanity of Pope had tempted him to intro-
duce himfelf. For this he had fome plaufible
colour; as with this Lady (who feems to have
been more *foolifh* than *unfortunate*, and to difcover whofe family and private hiftory Curiofity has laboured in vain) he had, or thought

L   it

it creditable to be thought to have had, some connexion in the way of friendship or love. The example of Pope has, in this instance, been imitated by Gray, who had not the same motive to inspire the design, nor the same ability to regulate the execution. In the abruptness of the introduction of their own affairs, and the want of art in engrafting them on the general design, there is a considerable similarity. The little Pope had to say of himself, he thought likely to come best from his own mouth. Gray, who has not said much more of himself, has put what is to be said in the mouth of another. Pope has alluded to his own death; but Gray, advancing a step farther, has proceeded to the circumstances of his burial, and even given us the epitaph on his stone.—Of this After-piece, rather *adhering* to the Elegy than uniting with it, Criticism thinks it unnecessary that the examination should be minute or long.

XXIV.

That a " *kindred* spirit." should be more interested in the fate of the writer, than one of a different temperament, is natural; but how this kindred spirit should, in his lonely

contem-

contemplations, ftumble into the fame Church-
yard in which this Elegy was written, we fearch
in vain for a probable account. One is tempted to fuppofe Gray to have fometimes figured
this Elegy as *fixed up* in the Country Church-
yard, as well as originally penned in it. But
this only leads us from one incongruity, to land
us immediately in another. Why does the
kindred fpirit enquire the fate of him, whofe
fate is commemorated in the Elegy that made
him originally known; as is alfo the very enquiry
he is here fuppofed to make. But I haften
from this part of the Piece, afraid of being involved in its entanglements, and apprehenfive
of the confufion of ideas that it feems to
threaten to him who fhall dwell on it long.

That Gray, in a work fo ferious, fhould have
intended to amufe himfelf, or his Reader, with
picturing the talkativenefs of the Ruftic Character, or the excurfivenefs of Narrative Age,
I am not willing to believe. But certain it is,
that the " hoary-headed fwain" tells the " kindred fpirit" more than was afked of him; and,
inftead of fimply relating the *fate* of the writer,
enters fomewhat diffufely into his *character*. Here,
again, the *manners* are violated; and the ruftic
is made to tell his tale, in language the moft
chafte and polifhed, and ftyle the moft poetical that the Elegy contains. Gray feems, by
a kind of perverfenefs of application, to have

finifhed

finished off this passage with all the care of
which he was master; and to have given it out
of his hand with a confcioufnefs of fuccefs, that
brings back to memory the felf-complacency of
Bayes, after one of his moft ranting paffages,
in which he thinks he has brought out every
excellence to which even *his* powers were ade-
quate—" *That* is as well as I *can* do."

That Gray fhould have formed a wifh to
exert himfelf with more than ordinary earneft-
nefs on a fubject fo near to him, is not to be
wondered at. But he forgets that the enthufiafm and fancy which might be allowable in
a defcription of his character, when that defcription came from himfelf, are inadmiffible
in the mouth of another, and that other a
ftranger, and a clown. But this is one of the
moft ftrongly marked peculiarities of his poetical
temperament. He is always more attentive to
the grandeur and magnificence of his building,
than to the propriety of its fite. He is ever
meditating a great ftructure; taking it for
granted, that it may ftand in all places alike.
From all quarters he fatigues himfelf in collect-
ing ponderous and bulky materials, which he
encourages himfelf to pile up till they fhall
have reached the Empyreum; without confidering the incongruities in the defign, or the ob-
ftacles that may ruin its execution: like the
commemorated projectors of a tower that was

to reach to heaven, which they began to build
in a plain, and without confidering that the
very laws of matter, on which the operation of
building proceeds, entailed impracticability on
their fcheme.—The epithet φιλοπονώ]αἰος, beſtow-
ed by an ancient Critick * on Euripides, may,
with propriety, be transferred to Gray; as may
alfo his defcription of the ſtrained and laboured elevation of that Poet's tragical imagery,
in which he is ludicroufly compared to Homer's
Lion, " laſhing his hips with his tail, and for-
" cing himfelf forward to fight."

XXV. XXVI. XXVII. XXVIII. XXIX.

Nor is much of the Poet's character unfolded
by the ruſtic; though many words are ufed.
" That he was a man given to muſing; that he
" loved to meet the fun in the morning, and to
" repofe in the ſhade at noon; that he walked by
" the fide of a wood, and lounged on the bank
" of a brook; and that, after having been two
" days a miffing, he was decently buried on the
" third at the foot of an old thorn"—is all that
the hoary-headed ſwain can fay about him:
for the reft he refers to the Epitaph, or, as he
calls it, the Lay, engraved upon his tomb-

* Longin. de Sublim.

ſtone;

ſtone; and which, from the kindred ſpirit's
knowing him by this Elegy, he doubts not he
is qualified to read.   Here is little gratification
to curioſity : and, as for the *original* queſtion
about his *fate*, we are left almoſt as much in
the dark as before.   That he is now dead and
buried, is all of his fate we know : though
the ſhortneſs of the interval between his burial,
and the time when he was laſt ſeen, with his
loitering ſo much by the ſide of the water, fur-
niſhes, in the caſe of ſo melancholy a man,
matter for further conjecture, and wakes ſuſ-
picion of *ſuicide.*

Of the three-ſtanza'd Epitaph, which the
ruſtic terms *a Lay*, the ſupplemental information
is not great.   " That he was poor, obſcure, pen-
" ſive, not unlearned, ſympathiſing, and bleſſed
" with a friend [I ſuppoſe of his own ſex], with
" ſomething more that might be mentioned,
" were it not unneceſſary to go deep into the
" character of a dead man"—is all the information we draw from it ; information not momentous enough to make us regret the want
of more.

The *manner* in which the character is " made
out," though in particular inſtances fortunate,
is not without faults.   The haſtineſs of his
ſteps in mounting " the upland lawn," and
the purpoſe for which he mounts it, are circumſtances more aſſociable with the *Allegro*
character,

character, than with the *Penserofo*. So thought the great Discriminator of these Characters. His Man of Cheerfulness is eager to observe the glory of the rising sun; his Pensive Man's morning is not bright, but " kerchief'd in a " comely cloud." —— So also Thomson, to whose authority, on most occasions, he has not scorned to pay some regard.

> As, through the falling glooms,
> Pensive I stray; *or*, with the rising dawn,
> On Fancy's eagle wing excursive soar *.

In Thomson these actions belong to *two* descriptions of character. Gray has wrought both into *one*. If the " steps" *must* be " hasty," the operation of brushing the dew from the grass will not help him to mend his pace; it is an action tending rather to impede accelerated motion, than promote it.

" Chance," in the twenty-fifth Stanza, used adverbially, though justified by a Latin idiom, is rebuting to an English ear. But the Poet was in distress. The necessity of his situation called for the idea twice within the compass of three lines. A word of two syllables brought him relief in the *one* case; and a word of *one* syllable in the other. He could not use " haply" twice. " Lonely contemplation," is not

* Summer.

well

well faid. Who is there that goes into company to contemplate? One is furprifed to fee a writer who deals in " trembling hope," " living afhes," " little great," put up fo contentedly with " folemn ftillnefs," " lonely contemplation," and " flowers that blow." Gray, fpeaking of water, has ufed " ambient tide." He that has dipt much in " ambient tide," will foon emerge to " ambient *air* :" then we fhall find him among " feathered fongfters ;" a fet of company rarely now to be met with even in Poetry's *horn-book*.

His " poring on the brook," is characteriftical. But his ftretching himfelf at the foot of a beech, is no more than the lounging Tityrus had done before him. Tityrus' beech is a fpreading one, as what beech is not? Of Gray's beech it is left to be fuppofed that it fpreads ; but we are exprefsly told that it *nods* ; and that it " wreathes its old fantaftic roots high." What is meant by a tree wreathing its roots high? Vegetation feems here inverted, and Age endowed with the pliancy of Youth.

Theory can in no other way account for the ftrange form in which this beech appears, than by fuppofing it to have been an image, not of Fancy, but of Fact. A mind ftrongly irritable upon the approximation of external forms, treafures up the grotefque images both of living

ing and ftill nature, as they prefent themfelves, and brings them forth afterwards as the effects of Infpiration. Gray had cafually come in the way of fome *lufus naturæ* of the beech tribe, of whofe fantaftic form the outline had continued upon his mind, and impreft his fancy with a vivid picture of it. Of Gray's infpirations, it is known, that many derived their origin from cafual impreffions, made on the organs of fenfe. The fight of the * Welch harper Parry; and the rapture he felt at his execution, animated him to the finifhing his *Bard,* after it had lain by for two years hopelefs: and the " loofe beard" and " hoary hair ftreaming " to the wind," with which he has invefted his tuneful Cambrian, were derived from a reprefentation, by Raphael, of the Supreme Being, in the vifion of Ezekiel †.

The beech feems *literally* to have been Gray's " favourite tree ;" and in the contemplation of it in all its varieties, he feems to have paffed many poetical hours. In the year 1737, he met with beeches, in grounds belonging to his uncle, of fo fingular a character, that I am willing to indulge the Reader the defcription of them in the Poet's own words ‡.

And, as they bow their hoary tops, relate,
In murmuring founds, the dark decrees of fate;
While *vifions,* as poetic eyes avow,
Cling to each leaf, and fwarm on every bough.

* Mafon.   † Ibid.   ‡ Ibid.

M   With

With such beeches he was fortunate enough
again to meet in Italy, after an interval of three
years; and them also he has celebrated, though
in the ancient language of their country *.

Hærent sub omni nam folio nigri
Phœbæa luci (credite) somnia;
Argutiusque et lympha et auræ
Nescio quid solito loquuntur †.

The thorn in Glastonbury church-yard is known
to have suggested to Gray, in the Elegy, the idea
of that *thorn*, under which he supposes himself to
be buried. What particular *beech* he had in his
eye, there is now no means of knowing. Chro-
nology forbids us to suppose it to have been the
beech which he found in the Highlands of Scot-
land, and which, to the astonishment of less
fortunate travellers, he reports, upon his own
mensuration, to have been *upwards of sixteen feet
in the girth, and no less than eighty feet high* ‡.

* Mason.

† Of visions *in fieri*, latent on the leaves of trees, till
poetic eyes shall *look them into form*, the conception, unless
borrowed from the Norse, may be new: though it was the
opinion of Dr. Blake, that the fancy of Gray was secretly
led, in the formation of it, by the obscure recollection of
the Legend of Sir John Mandeville, according to which,
in certain very cold latitudes, articulate sounds were arrested
by the frost, at the moment of their emission from the
mouth of the speaker, and continued in that torpid state,
until they were again *thawed into vocality*, by the return
of the warm season.

‡ Mason.

9

Why the Penfive Man fhould lie rather under the fhade of a beech, than under any
other fhady tree, except Gray's predilection for
the beech, no reafon can be affigned. In a
fituation nearly fimilar, Thomfon ftretches himfelf under an *oak*. The *general idea* is the fame.

—— Let me hafte into the mid-wood fhade,
Where fcarce a fun-beam wanders thro' the gloom ;
And, on the dark green grafs, *befide the brink*
Of haunted ftream, that by the roots of OAK
Rolls o'er the rocky channel, lie at large *.

XXX. XXXI. XXXII.

Of the *Epitaph* much more need not be faid.
The head of him who is immerfed in earth,
can with little propriety be faid to reft *on her*
lap. The transference of the word *lap*, is not
happy. It is " velvet green" over again.
The ground of the objection is the fame. A
metaphor drawn from Nature ennobles Art.
A metaphor drawn from Art degrades Nature.
As Gray is known to have been learned, that
" Science frowned not on his birth," may be
faid with truth, according to the ufual accept-
ation of the words. But phrafes, fuch as
" Fortune fmiled on his birth," " Science

* Summer.

M 2   " frown'd

" frown'd not on his birth," are become flat by ufage. They *were* poetical; are *now* rhetorical; and will *foon* be profaic.

He who gives to Mifery all he has," when that all is a tear, may be free'd from the charge of hard-heartednefs; but will be affectedly denominated bountiful; as his giving *this kind of all,* will be with quaintnefs called *giving largely.* " Recompence" is ufed improperly. For lofs or fuffering we make recompence, but for bounty we offer *return*: and we are not properly faid to " difclofe" that, which by inveftigation we *difcover.* " Merits " and frailties repofing on the bofom of his " father, and his God," is an idea which Apprehenfion doubts if fhe has clearly made out: but, if " Father" and " God" relate to the fame Being, the idea is pious, and the Elegy ends better than it begun. Meditation guides to Morality; Morality infpires Religion; and Religion fwells out into devotion.

It is furprifing that a writer like Gray fhould think the authority of Petrarch neceffary to the juftification of the expreffion, " trembling " hope;" an expreffion, which, though it has a little of the *concetto* in it, has it in lefs degree than feveral others he has ufed without fcruple. But Gray was fond of Petrarch, and had no objection that his fondnefs fhould be known.

In

In his Notes he is oftentatious of authorities in the defence of his expreſſions. Had it become expedient for him, on any occaſion, to uſe the "joy of grief," he would no doubt have referred his Reader to the Pſeudo-Gallic Poems, which, at a particular time, he wrought up his fancy to reliſh, and almoſt his underſtanding to believe authentic.——On the preſent occaſion, there was no need to travel ſo far as Petrarch for an authority; for what is the mode of ſpeaking or writing that will not have its authority in the compoſitions of every language. Pope's "trembling, hoping," was at hand. Even the copartenery of Tate and Brady would have furniſhed him with "awful mirth."

Of the.* Stanza that Gray once publiſhed as part of this Elegy, and afterwards ſaw cauſe to withdraw, Criticiſm chooſes to decline the examination, unwilling to ſhew eagerneſs to condemn him, who has already condemned himſelf. For the diſcontinuance of it in the after-editions, Maſon has aſſigned this cauſe, that it was thought by its Author to be awkwardly parenthetical. But there were other reaſons that rendered it expedient that it ſhould

---

* There, ſcatter'd oft, the earlieſt of the year,
  By hands unſeen, are ſhow'rs of violets found;
  The Red-breaſt loves to build and warble there,
  And little footſteps lightly print the ground.

be fuffered to *flip out* quietly. The fame images, delineated and affembled nearly in the fame manner, are to be found in fome of Collins' Pieces, publifhed about 1746. I am aware that to fix imitation upon Gray, is not to beftow originality upon Collins. Some of Collins' images can be traced to Pope; and fome of Pope's, as well as Collins', to ages of high antiquity. " By foreign hands thy dying eyes " were clofed, &c." make part of the wailings of Electra in Sophocles, for the fuppofed death of Oreftes: " The turf lying light on the breaft," (to which a ludicrous contraft is on record) ftanding now fo high in the lift of elegiac common places, occurs in the Alceftis of Euripides; and Homer has made his Mountain Nymphs (the Fays of thofe times) plant elms, fince converted into flowers, around Eetion's grave. Property in fancy is like other property. Priority of appropriation muft found the original right; and of that priority our inveftigation muft determine with the Record.

Of the writers to whom Gray has done homage for his tenure, I think Pope is not one. Let it not however be imagined, that, though nothing is acknowledged, nothing is owing. The " Elegy to the Memory of an unfortunate " Lady," has given to the " Elegy written in a " Country Church-yard," many things both in the way of fentiment and defign.

The

The "ftoried urn" of Gray, is the "weep-
"ing Loves" of Pope: and "animated buft,"
is only an obfcure expreffion for Pope's "po-
"lifhed marble emulating the face."

What though no facred earth allow the room,
Nor hallowed dirge be mutter'd o'er thy tomb,

has furnifhed the perhaps improved idea expreffed in

Tho' Mem'ry o'er their tomb no trophies raife,
Where thro' the long-drawn aile and fretted vault,
The pealing anthem fwells the note of praife.

That funeral honours, however fcrupuloufly
paid, cannot "back from its manfion call the
"fleeting breath," is alfo to be found in Pope,
though ftated in a different way :

So peaceful refts without a ftone, a name,
What once had beauty, titles, wealth and fame ;—
A heap of duft alone remains of thee:
'Tis all thou art ; *and all the* PROUD *fhall be.*

"The Morn beftowing her earlieft tears;"
(poetical language for dew) "the *firft* rofes of
"the year blowing, &c." are images which
both Collins and Gray thought worth gather-
ing.

* * * * * * * * * *

Here Criticifm is content to ftop : congra-
tulating herfelf on the termination of a labour
irkfome,

irkfome, but not overwhelming; invidious, but not void of ufe. If fhe has defcended into too minute an examination, it has not been with a view to darken counfel, but to furnifh light. Of fine writjng, the perfection is not fo well promoted by abftract canons, as by individual illuftrations; by the inculcating what *fhould be* written, as by the examination of what *has*. The detection of particular blemifhes, is more productive than the difplay of general perfection. There is a common-weal in tafte, as well as in government. Minute and charaacteriftical exhibitions, of errors as well as of excellence, are neceffary for improvement, in both. *Inde tibi, tuæque* REIPUBLICÆ, *quod imitere, capias; inde fædum* INCEPTU, *fædum* EXITU, *quod vites.* In the execution of this neceffary tafk, Criticifm finds herfelf engaged in much labour, and fubjected to much felf-denial: impeded by Prejudice, and thruft back by Mifconftruction. But the labour is honourable; and the end ufeful. She is content to forget the hardfhips fhe has fuffered; and folace herfelf with the view of the good fhe has done.

In examining the Elegy written in a Country Church-yard, fhe has found much room for cenfure, and fome room for praife. The Piece has been much over-rated; and many ferious perfons, who meditate on death from a fenfe

of

of duty, confider Confcience as concerned in
their finding *this* Meditation *perfect*. Of perfections no doubt it contains fome; .but it
contains blemifhes too; and if Criticifm grant
it nothing but its merit, what then will be its
praife ?

To *rate* that merit precifely, is perhaps not
eafy : but, where the premifes are, the con-
clufion may be found. Thofe who are refolved
to fortify themfelves in the feeling they have
encouraged themfelves to entertain of its perfections, may find many ftrong pofitions, in
which they may maintain themfelves, without immediate danger of being *forced*. The
fubject is ferious; the views interefting; the
thoughts tender; the verfification, in general,
fmooth; the language not unfuitable. ——
The flights are fometimes bold; often catching:
and the execution often ftriking; and fometimes
natural. But what, of all things, is likely
to enfure this Performance a lafting and general Intereft is, that it abounds with images
which find a mirrour in every mind, and with
fentiments to which every bofom returns an
echo. Where fo many beauties are, room
may be afforded for faults : of thefe, Criticifm
has not concealed what came in her way; and
to fuch as may urge her to a farther fearch,

N   fhe

fhe will content herfelf with tendering, concerning the Elegy, the admonition which its
Writer has tendered concerning himfelf :

NO FARTHER SEEK ITS MERITS TO DISCLOSE,
NOR DRAW ITS FRAILTIES FROM THEIR DREAD
ABODE.

F I N I S.

www.ingramcontent.com/pod-product-compliance
Lightning Source LLC
Chambersburg PA
CBHW022341020726
47500CB00004B/1220